Open access edition supported by the National Endowment for the Humanities /
Andrew W. Mellon Foundation Humanities Open Book Program.

© 2019 Johns Hopkins University Press
Published 2019

Johns Hopkins University Press
2715 North Charles Street
Baltimore, Maryland 21218-4363
www.press.jhu.edu

ISBN-13: 978-1-4214-3659-3 (open access)
ISBN-10: 1-4214-3659-0 (open access)

ISBN-13: 978-1-4214-3657-9 (pbk. : alk. paper)
ISBN-10: 1-4214-3657-4 (pbk. : alk. paper)

ISBN-13: 978-1-4214-3658-6 (electronic)
ISBN-10: 1-4214-3658-2 (electronic)

This page supersedes the copyright page included in the original publication of this work.

THE JOHNS HOPKINS HISTORICAL
PUBLICATIONS

THE SCOURGE OF THE CLERGY
PETER OF DREUX, DUKE OF BRITTANY

BY

SIDNEY PAINTER

1969

OCTAGON BOOKS

New York

Reprinted 1969
by special arrangement with The Johns Hopkins Press

OCTAGON BOOKS
A DIVISION OF FARRAR, STRAUS & GIROUX, INC.
19 Union Square West
New York, N. Y. 10003

AM

LIBRARY OF CONGRESS CATALOG CARD NUMBER: 76-96188

Printed in U.S.A. by
TAYLOR PUBLISHING COMPANY
DALLAS, TEXAS

PREFACE

This book has been written because I wanted to write it. I first met Peter of Dreux in the pages of Henry Adams' *Mont-Saint-Michel and Chartres,* and my interest in him ripened into fascination as I read more deeply into the historical literature dealing with thirteenth-century France. But my personal relish for the details of the stormy career of this baron is hardly sufficient justification for inflicting another book on the overburdened shelves of our libraries. Fortunately, however, it is always easy to produce plausible rationalizations in support of what one wishes to do. Any reasonably competent historian who works over the material used by his predecessors should be able to make some additions to the sum of historical knowledge. I believe that I have made several definite contributions to our knowledge of the years covered by the life of Peter of Dreux, but the points which I hope I have elucidated will be of interest primarily to specialists in the history of France and Brittany during this period. The principal justification for the publication of this biography must be sought in its possible didactic value. Many people who are interested in thirteenth-century France have read vague general accounts of the development of the great feudal states, the struggles between the French kings and their vassals, the rivalry of the Capetian and Plantagenet monarchies, the quarrels between church and state, and the crusades of St. Louis. All these and many other phases of the history of the first half of the thirteenth century are concretely illustrated by the career of Peter of Dreux. Finally if my artistic competence has been equal to the task set before it, the reader will share my enthusiasm for Peter himself. Even if he had not played an important rôle in the political life of his day, his personality would have made him a worthy subject for a biography.

Several years after I started to gather material for a life of Peter of Dreux, I learned that a contemporary of mine, the French scholar Jacques Levron, was engaged on the same task.

In addition to several articles M. Levron has published a *Catalogue des actes de Pierre de Dreux, duc de Bretagne* and *Pierre Mauclerc, duc de Bretagne*. Although the latter appeared in two sections in the *Mémoires de la société d'histoire et d'archéologie de Bretagne,* it is a formal biography of over two hundred pages. In my fourth appendix I have given some illustrations of M. Levron's competence as a historian, and I believe that it is fair to say that they are typical of his work as a whole. I am glad, however, to be able to acknowledge my indebtedness to him for a number of documents which I might well have missed.

While full responsibility for the deficiencies of this biography must rest solely upon me, I must share the credit for its good qualities with my colleagues and students in the department of history of The Johns Hopkins University. I am particularly indebted to Professor Kent Roberts Greenfield for the time and effort which he devoted to reading and criticizing the manuscript. The staffs of the libraries of The Johns Hopkins, Princeton, and Yale Universities, of the Peabody Institute, and of the Library of Congress have been unfailingly helpful in supplying the books needed for my research. The officials of the Archives nationales in Paris have contributed much to the ease of my work by their prompt and courteous compliance with requests for photostats of unpublished documents. Finally I wish to express my gratitude to Professor Ernst Cloos and Miss Lucille Havens who drew and lettered the map which accompanies this volume and to Mrs. Victoria Golz who assisted me in reading the proof.

TABLE OF CONTENTS

I

A DUCHESS' HUSBAND

Hopeful Young Knight

On Whitsunday of the year 1209 in the royal town of Compiègne Philip Augustus, king of France, bestowed the dignity of knighthood on three young men of Capetian blood— his own son and heir, Louis, and Robert and Peter, sons of his cousin Count Robert of Dreux.[1] This solemn ceremony admitted the three youths to the positions to which their birth entitled them in the chivalry of France. The thirteenth century knew no more exalted social group nor one offering greater opportunities to talented young men than the feudal caste which ruled the land of the *langue d'oi*. From Stirling bridge to the south coast of Sicily, from the river Clare to beyond the Jordan, the knights of France were noted for their hardihood and prowess in battle. The Latin empire of Constantinople, the kingdom of Jerusalem, and the kingdom of Cyprus were ruled by French barons. A strong Norman strain ran in the blood of the king and aristocracy of Sicily and Naples. The noble houses of western France had furnished England with its monarch and baronage. Even as they gathered about their sovereign at Compiègne the barons of northern France were planning the conquest of their neighbors to the south who had shown themselves too tolerant toward the Albigensian heretics.[2] The same military ardor which gave the French aristocracy its dominant position in thirteenth-century Europe made its home-

---

[1] Johannes Longus, *Chronica monasterii Sancti Bertini, Recueil des historiens des Gaules et de la France*, XVIII, 603. *Chronique d'un anonyme de Béthune, ibid.*, XXIV, 763. Guillaume le Breton, *Gesta Philippi Augusti*, in *Oeuvres de Rigord et de Guillaume le Breton* (ed. H. F. Delaborde, *Société de l'histoire de France*, Paris, 1882-1885), I, 226.

[2] Ch. Petit-Dutaillis, *Étude sur la vie et le règne de Louis VIII* (Paris, 1894), p. 25.

land the center for tournaments and all knightly sports. The religious zeal which combined with their love of fighting and greed for fiefs to send the nobles of France against the infidel had sown their domains with monastic foundations. But while they were the first knights of Europe and the most favored sons of the church, these men no longer accepted the simple Christian warriors of the *Chanson de Roland* as their model of chivalric perfection. The cult of Courtly Love with its romances and lyric poetry had not softened the chivalry of France, but it had diversified its interests. The rhyming baron was to be a common figure in thirteenth-century France. Thus Peter of Dreux when he received the belt of knighthood from his royal kinsman became a member of a class that was not only rich and powerful but pleasant and cultivated as well.

Despite his royal blood this young knight seemed destined for a comparatively humble position in the social group into which he had been born. The day of extensive appanages for the cadets of the ruling house had not yet come when Louis VI of France endowed his second son, Robert. The county of Dreux was a small fief on the border of Normandy. To this Count Robert I had added by marriage the county of Braine to the northeast of Paris which his descendants held as vassals of the counts of Champagne. These two counties with a few scattered fiefs were the entire patrimony of the house of Dreux. In a society where feudal power meant far more than high birth Peter's father, Count Robert II, was of no great importance. Northern France, the land of the *langue d'oi,* was ruled by five dynasties of feudal princes—the Capetian kings, the dukes of Burgundy and Brittany, and the counts of Champagne and Flanders. Far below these potentates stood the highest rank of their vassals composed of men who held the comptal title but whose domains were small and vassals few. There among barons like the counts of Blois, Chartres, and Nevers were the peers of Count Robert of Dreux. As a cadet of his house Peter would have to be content with a few small fiefs held from his elder brother—the castles and towns of Fère-en-Tardenois and Brie-Comte-Robert and the petty manors of

Chilly and Longjumeau.[3] He would be a minor baron of Champagne and the Ile-de-France.

Although Count Robert II lacked extensive fiefs, he had other assets which were to be of immense benefit to his sons. He was the head of a large and powerful family, and he enjoyed the confidence and friendship of King Philip. By judicious marriages the house of Dreux had become allied with most of the barons who ruled between the rivers Marne and Somme. The most powerful lord of this region, the able, arrogant, and ruthlessly ambitious Enguerrand III of Coucy, was Peter's cousin. Mathew II, lord of Montmorency and constable of France, was his cousin by marriage.[4] In an age when blood relationship was a peculiarly potent bond such connections were of great value to a young man. But the real strength of the house of Dreux lay in its cordial relations with the senior branch of the Capetian family. Count Robert had all the qualities of the perfect vassal. In him bravery, prowess, and love of knightly sports were combined with gentle piety, political docility, and absolute loyalty to his royal cousin. His brother, Philip of Dreux, bishop of Beauvais, a fierce warrior prelate far more at home with the sword than with the pastoral staff, had earned his king's gratitude for distinguished service rendered in the Norman marches during the long struggle with the Plantagenets. Both close kinship and appreciation of loyal service inclined King Philip to benevolence toward the house of Dreux.

The friendship of Philip Augustus was Peter's greatest asset. The favor of kings was absolutely essential to an ambitious younger son who hoped to attain a high position in the feudal world. No longer was there much opportunity for a man of energy and ability to win a rich fief by the sword. Even in the border lands of European civilization—Wales, Ireland, the Iberian peninsula, and the Orient—society was too well stabilized to leave room for the fief-hungry warrior. Peter might

---

[3] *Layettes du trésor des chartes* (ed. Alexandre Teulet, Paris, 1863-1866), II, no. 1720. *Cartulaire de l'église Notre-Dame de Paris* (ed. Guérard, Paris, 1850), II, 262. *Gallia Christiana in provincias ecclesiasticas distributa* (Paris, 1715-1765), VII, 863.

[4] See genealogical table no. 1.

envy the astounding success of Geoffrey de Villehardoin, but he could have little hope of being able to emulate him. While high competence in feudal politics combined with unusual military ability might enable him to add a few small fiefs to his patrimony, he would live and die a minor baron. But feudal custom did provide one path to the possession of a large fief—marriage to a rich heiress. While every well-born and impecunious young man dreamed of wedding the eldest daughter of an important baron, Peter might well hope that his dreams would materialize. The hands of all the more desirable heiresses were at the disposal of the crown, and he had reason to count on the good will of King Philip.

Unfortunately, however, the very qualities which were to make Peter a dominant figure in western Europe placed him at a serious disadvantage as a candidate for the hand of the mistress of a major fief. A sharp-featured young man already noted for prowess in battle, he was able, determined, ambitious, and turbulent.[5] Like his uncle the warrior bishop of Beauvais he had inherited the traits of his great-grandfather, Louis VI, rather than those of the gentle, obedient, and pliant counts of Dreux. King Philip had devoted thirty years to curbing the power of the feudal potentates, and he was inclined to consider docility as the most desirable characteristic of a vassal. Affection for the house of Dreux might move him to give Peter an heiress of secondary importance, but he was unlikely to place so forceful a young man at the head of one of the great feudal states. Hence Peter was obliged to watch two highly covetable heiresses being bestowed on other men. Alix, duchess of Brittany, was affianced to her kinsman Henry, son of Count Alan of Tréguier and Lamballe. As Alix was nine years old and her fiancé four, Philip was certain that they would give him no trouble.[6] The heiress of a still richer fief,

---

[5] The sharp features were mentioned by Thibaut of Champagne. *Les chansons de Thibaut de Champagne, roi de Navarre* (ed. A. Wallensköld, *Société des anciens textes français*, Paris, 1925), no. 40, line 62; no. 50, line 8.

[6] *Mémoires pour servir de preuves à l'histoire ecclésiastique et civile de Bretagne* (ed. Dom Hyacinthe Morice, Paris, 1742-1746), I, 812-813. Bertrand de Broussillon, *La maison de Laval* (Paris, 1895-1903), I, 299. Arthur de la Borderie, *Histoire de Bretagne* (Rennes, 1896-1914), III, 297.

Jeanne, countess of Flanders, was given to a foreign prince, Ferrand of Portugal. Clearly King Philip had no desire to see a man of Peter's character duke of Brittany or count of Flanders.

Fortunately for Peter the next three years saw a complete change in the political situation. In 1209 Philip contemplated the gradual destruction of the great vassals of the crown and the concentration of all princely authority in the king's person; in 1212 he feared the absolute nullification of the triumphs of his reign. When Philip ascended the throne of France in 1180, he had found himself master of the Ile-de-France, the Orleanais, and the Gâtinais—a petty region which was barely equal in financial and military resources to the domains of the count of Flanders or the count of Champagne and far inferior to those of the Plantagenet ruler of Normandy, Maine, Anjou, Touraine, and Aquitaine who held in addition the kingdom of England. King Philip had succeeded in altering the balance of power between the crown and the count of Flanders by depriving the latter of the Artois district, but his greatest achievement had been the conquest of Normandy, Maine, Anjou, Touraine, and Poitou from King John of England. The acquisition of Normandy alone would have given the Capetian monarch a dominant position in northern France. The revenues of this great duchy in the early thirteenth century were roughly equal to those of the Capetian domains after the acquisition of Artois and to those of the English realm. Thus the conquest of Normandy almost doubled the financial resources of the French crown and reduced proportionately the power of its most dangerous rival. Without Normandy the Capetian king was the equal of his great vassals; with it he had only to fear a well-organized baronial league. But King John was determined to recover his continental fiefs. In 1211 he formed a close alliance with his nephew Otto, Holy Roman Emperor, and the German princes of the Rhine valley. Two of the chief vassals of the French crown, the count of Flanders who mourned the loss of Artois and the count of Toulouse who resented Philip's encouragement of the Albigensian crusaders, were members of this league. Many barons of the lands which Philip had taken from his Plantagenet foe knew that if John

were victorious they could regain their fiefs in England and
hence were inclined to favor the cause of their former master.
If the French monarchy was to retain the ground which it had
gained during the vigorous reign of King Philip, it would need
powerful and able friends.

In any contest between the kings of France and England the
duchy of Brittany was bound to be of immense strategic importance. Its hardy mariners menaced the sea-route from England
to Poitou and Gascony, while its long eastern frontier adjoined
the former Plantagenet domains north of the river Loire. If
Brittany had been actively loyal, King Philip would have had
little to fear from an English invasion. But from this point of
view the situation in the duchy was far from encouraging. The
father of the Duchess Alix, Guy of Thouars, who ruled as regent for his young daughter, was a man of little force and
almost no influence in Brittany. Moreover he had supported
King John in his last invasion of France, and his brother,
Aimery VII, viscount of Thouars, a notorious turncoat, was at
the moment an adherent of the English king. Even more disturbing was the fact that the rights of the Duchess Alix were
far from incontestable. Guy of Thouars had been the third
husband of Constance, duchess of Brittany. Eleanor, daughter
of Constance by her first husband, Geoffrey Plantagenet, still
lived in an English prison, and this sister of the murdered
Arthur was, in default of heirs male, the rightful duchess of
Brittany instead of her younger half-sister. Ever since Arthur's
disappearance a party in the Breton baronage had been nego-
tiating with John for Eleanor's release.[7] Early in 1212 an important lord of western Brittany, Hervé, viscount of Léon, had
a safe-conduct to visit John in England.[8] It is impossible to
say how large Eleanor's following was, how serious were its
intentions, nor how much Philip knew of its activities, but the
fact that John when he invaded France in 1214 carried Eleanor
with him seems to indicate that he had hopes of winning strong
Breton support through her. If Alix's position was to be maintained and the resources of her duchy used effectively to support

[7] *Rotuli litterarum patentium* (ed. T. D. Hardy, *Record commission*), pp. 67,
91b. See genealogical chart no. 2.
[8] *Ibid.*, p. 93.

the Capetian cause, Brittany would have to be placed under a loyal, capable, and forceful duke. The duchess' fiancé, seven-year-old Henry of Tréguier, was obviously too young for such a task. Reluctantly, and fully realizing the risks he was taking, King Philip turned toward Peter of Dreux. There lay strength and energy, but hardly docility.

Although the emergency which confronted him was forcing Philip to give the duchy of Brittany to a man whom he considered dangerous, he was far too wary a monarch to neglect any precautions which might prevent Peter from becoming a serious menace to the authority of the crown. The power of a feudal prince depended on the effectiveness of his control over his own vassals and his alliances with his fellows. King Philip's life-long policy had been to support the vassals of the great fiefs in their contests with their lords and to break up all baronial leagues. In pursuing this course against Guy of Thouars the king had created in Brittany a strong francophile party headed by Alan, count of Tréguier and Lamballe, and André II, lord of Vitré. Hence he was determined to do his best to prevent Peter from increasing the ducal authority at the expense of the independence of the Breton barons. Furthermore, he wished to avoid the formation of a league between the new duke of Brittany and his relatives of the house of Dreux. In November 1212 Peter was obliged to swear that he would observe all agreements made by .the king with Guy of Thouars and his barons and that he would deprive no baron of Brittany of lands or privileges without a decision of Philip's court. His father Count Robert, his uncle Bishop Philip of Beauvais, and his elder brother Robert of Dreux solemnly promised that they would not aid him in any way against the king.[9] On January 27, 1213, Peter did liege homage to King Philip for the duchy of Brittany. He agreed that he should accept the homages of the Breton barons only on the understanding that if he violated his promises they would support Philip against him.[10] If solemn oaths could bind Peter, the king had succeeded in making him

[9] *Layettes*, I, nos. 601, 1026, 1027. No. 601 is dated 1200 by Teulet, but it obviously belongs with nos. 1026 and 1027. Teulet disregarded a redundant *ducentissimo* instead of correcting it to *duodecimo*.
[10] *Ibid.*, no. 1033.

innocuous. But clearly Philip himself had doubts as to their efficacy. As a more practical precautionary measure he married Alix's younger sister Catherine to the new head of the franco-phile house of Vitré, young André III.[11]

Shortly after Peter had performed his homage to Philip Augustus, he issued a charter in which he styled himself *dux Britonum*.[12] This prompt assumption of the title of duke was most significant. The position of the lord of Brittany in the feudal hierarchy of France was highly ambiguous. His domains were as extensive as those of the count of Flanders and his real power as great as that of the count of Toulouse. He shared with the duke of Burgundy the honor of being at least in theory the leader of a distinct people. Yet he was not like these barons a peer of France.[13] The explanation of this situation probably lies in the fact that during the years in which the conception of the peerage was taking form the master of Brittany was a vassal of the Norman dukes. While Peter's immediate predecessors, Arthur Plantagenet and Guy of Thouars, had done homage to Philip Augustus, the propriety of their position as direct vassals of the French crown depended on the legality of Philip's confiscation of King John's continental fiefs. In short the lord of Brittany was a vassal of Philip, duke of Normandy, rather than of Philip, king of France. Hence like the barons of Normandy, Maine, Anjou, and Poitou he could reasonably claim that the English king was his natural suzerain and had a right to his homage whenever he could protect him.[14] Furthermore, the Breton dukes were by inheritance lords of the great English barony of Richmond which had been seized by King John when they transferred their allegiance to the French crown.[15] The geographical position of Brittany, its long dependence on the

[11] *Cartulaire de Laval et de Vitré*, in Broussillon, *Maison de Laval*, nos. 318-320. This will be referred to as *Cartulaire de Vitré*.

[12] *Ibid.*, no. 321.

[13] There were at this time six lay peerages—the duchies of Aquitaine, Burgundy, and Normandy and the counties of Champagne, Flanders, and Toulouse. See François de Valon, *Les pairs de France primitifs et leur cour* (Toulouse, 1931).

[14] See the letter of the viscount of Limoges to King Philip in 1214. *Rot. pat.*, p. 115. He speaks of John as *naturali domino meo*.

[15] *Ibid.*, p. 51.

Anglo-Norman and Plantagenet kings, and its duke's interests in England tended to make it a border region between the Capetian and Plantagenet monarchies. The natural policy of the French king was to ignore the Breton claim to be an independent people, to sever Brittany's connections with England, and to deny its lord the status of a peer of France. The question of the title to be borne by Peter was purely symbolic, but symbolism was of great importance in the thirteenth century. A duke who was not a peer with all the authority and independence which that dignity implied was inconceivable. To Philip and his successors Peter was count of Brittany.[16] Despite the extent and importance of his fief he ranked in the feudal hierarchy with the secondary barons like the counts of Dreux. But in this earliest of his charters Peter gave notice that he would not accept this classification. He was *dux Britonum*, the chief of the Bretons, the title which was preferred by those who believed in the rights of the people of Brittany.[17] While he did not long retain this appellation which was more romantic than practical, he exchanged it for one even more provocative. By May 1213 his acts bore the heading "Peter, duke of Brittany and earl of Richmond."[18] Not only was he a duke, but he intended to maintain his claim to the English lands of his wife's house.

It is unlikely that his protegé's attitude either surprised or disturbed King Philip. He had made his choice when he gave the heiress of Brittany to his able and ambitious young cousin. While the king might hope that chivalric respect for the man

[16] The French and papal chanceries always addressed Peter as count. The English did the same until 1226. After that he was always formally addressed as duke of Brittany and earl of Richmond, but he was still often referred to as count of Brittany. Most chroniclers spoke of him as count. A striking exception was William the Breton who called him *dux Britonum*. I know only one act of Peter's in which he used the title count of Brittany, and that was probably drawn up in the English chancery. *Patent rolls, 1216-1225 (Rolls series)*, p. 174. He did, however, sometimes refer to himself as count. See letter printed in appendix I.

[17] Guillaume le Breton, *Gesta, Oeuvres*, I, 255, 298; *Philippidos, ibid.*, II, 256, 268. But even William could slip into count. *Gesta*, p. 251.

[18] Arthur de la Borderie, "Recueil d'actes inédits des ducs et princes de Bretagne," *Mémoires de la société archéologique d'Ille et Vilaine*, XVII (1885), nos. 83, 85. This work was published separately under the same title at Rennes in 1888. It will be referred to as *Recueil*.

who had dubbed him a knight and gratitude for the gift of a rich fief would tend to keep Peter loyal and obedient, he must have been enough of a realist to understand that the new duke's policy would be governed essentially by his conception of his own best interests. No vassal would hesitate to extend his own authority at the expense of his suzerain's if he could do so with impunity, and few barons had any scruples against transferring their allegiance to a new lord if that seemed the most profitable course. The thirteenth century knew no theory of nationalism that decreed that Peter as a Frenchman should devote himself to the interests of the French king. The place of national feeling was occupied by the conception of the natural lord—that is, the traditional one—and this urged the duke of Brittany toward allegiance to the king of England. While Peter kept a firm grip on his vassals and held John and his allies at bay, Peter would be reasonably obedient and loyal. If baronial turbulence or foreign foes should triumph, Peter would make common cause with the victors. Meantime he would strive to increase his power and authority as best he might.

Tortuous Path to Richmond

Peter's first visit to his new fief was very brief. On April 8, 1213, he attended at Soissons the council which Philip had summoned to plan an attack on John before the latter's German allies should be ready to strike.[19] The English king was excommunicate, and Pope Innocent III had authorized Philip to drive him from his kingdom. Early in May Peter was in Brittany raising money to support his contingent in the army which was mustering for the invasion of England.[20] By the middle of the same month he must have been in the royal host at Boulogne. But the projected invasion of England was abortive. John made peace with the church, and Pandulf, the papal legate, forbade Philip to attack him. Furiously angry at what he considered papal perfidy, the French king turned his army against Count Ferrand of Flanders who had openly shown his

[19] Guillaume le Breton, *Philippidos, Oeuvres*, II, 256.
[20] *Recueil*, no. 83.

treason by refusing to obey the summons to the host. Peter accompanied Philip on this expedition and led the vanguard of the royal army when it repulsed the raid of Earl William of Salisbury and the count of Boulogne.[21]

The real test of the soundness of King Philip's judgment in placing Peter in control of Brittany came in the summer of 1214. In that year the great coalition launched its long-planned attack. John was to invade France from Poitou, while the Emperor Otto in command of a large allied army advanced from the north. Philip's plan was to concentrate his main force against the imperial host while his son Louis and the local barons held John as best they could. The English king landed at La Rochelle in mid-February and spent the next few months solidifying his position in Poitou. The Poitevin barons, headed by the Lusignans and the viscount of Thouars, joined his camp with their usual nonchalance. By the end of May John was ready to strike at the Loire valley. Leaving Parthenay on May 28 he marched near enough to Moncontour to force Louis, who was besieging the castle, to withdraw to Chinon and then turned north toward the Loire. On June 5 he occupied Pirmel which lay on the south bank of the river opposite Nantes.[22] This city, the chief place of Brittany and the key to the lower Loire valley, was held by Peter and his Breton levies reinforced by a party of French knights under his brother Robert.

Considering the fact that Nantes was well-nigh impregnable on the south where it was covered by the Loire, one cannot but wonder why John chose to advance on it from that direction.

---

[21] Guillaume le Breton, *Gesta, Oeuvres*, I, 251-252; *Philippidos, ibid.*, II, 268-269.

[22] *Rotuli litterarum clausarum* (ed. T. D. Hardy, *Record commission*), I, 166-167. *Rot. pat.*, pp. 116-117. John's itinerary between May 28 and June 11 has given historians much trouble because of the difficulty of identifying the places mentioned on the rolls. On May 29 he was at *Chichy* which must have been Chiché halfway between Parthenay and Moncontour. On June 2, 3, and 4 he was at *Spina* which is unidentifiable except that it was clearly near Ancenis as on June 11 John issued letters at both places. On June 5 and 6 the king was at *Pilem*. Cartellieri identified this as Pirmel. His very convincing reasons are strengthened by the fact that in 1230 Henry III issued letters at *Pilem* on his way from Nantes to Montaigu. *Patent rolls, 1225-1232*, p. 382. *Close rolls, 1227-1231 (Rolls series)*, p. 417. See Alexander Cartellieri, *Philipp II August, König von Frankreich* (Leipzig, 1899-1921), IV, 418.

The answer undoubtedly lies in his thorough comprehension of the temptations which were facing Peter. He had just acquired a magnificent feudal position and had no desire to lose it. The presence of Eleanor of Brittany in John's camp clearly suggested Peter's fate if the English were victorious.[23] The French cause looked desperate. Would it not be wise to follow the example of his wife's uncle, Viscount Aimery of Thouars, and join the English standard? Furthermore he could hardly ignore the rich bribe which John could dangle before his eyes—the honor of Richmond. In 1215 the English king was to offer it to Peter in return for his aid against his rebellious barons.[24] While there is no positive evidence that he made a similar offer in 1214, it is hardly conceivable that he would have been less generous when the success of his long-planned continental campaign was at stake. In short John occupied Pirmel because he hoped to be admitted to Nantes and receive the submission of the duke of Brittany.

If John really expected Peter to be so crude as to commit open and obvious treason at so early a stage in the campaign, he was sorely mistaken. When the English and Poitevin army appeared at Pirmel, the two Dreux brothers sallied out from the barbican at the head of the bridge leading to Nantes and drove in John's advance guard. Peter then discreetly retired, but Robert pressed too near John's main force and was captured with some score of his knights.[25] This little skirmish satisfied the king's curiosity. He was not to gain free admittance to Nantes and must seek his passage over the Loire elsewhere. Moving slowly up the river he crossed either at Oudon or Ancenis—probably at the former place. By June 11 he had captured both these towns.[26] The comparative speed with which John reduced these two formidable Breton fortresses leads one

---

[23] Eleanor's presence is attested by Ralph of Coggeshall, *Chronicon Anglicanum* (ed. Joseph Stevenson, *Rolls series*), p. 168.

[24] *Rot. pat.*, p. 152b.

[25] Roger of Wendover, *Flores historiarum* (ed. H. G. Hewlett, *Rolls series*), II, 104. *Histoire des ducs de Normandie et des rois d'Angleterre* (ed. F. Michel, *Société de l'histoire de France*, Paris, 1840), p. 143. Guillaume le Breton, *Gesta, Oeuvres*, I, 254-255; *Philippidos, ibid.*, II, 283.

[26] *Rot. claus.*, I, 167. *Rot. pat.*, p. 117. Guillaume le Breton, *Gesta, Oeuvres*, I, 254.

to suspect Peter's enthusiasm for the French cause. While the vassal who actually held Ancenis and Oudon may have submitted without his suzerain's approval, it is rather unlikely that he did. Certainly Peter made no serious attempt to hold these towns by moving up the north bank of the Loire as John advanced on the southern one. The duke's position is rendered still more equivocal by the fact that Judicael de Guérande, a rich merchant of Nantes, was carrying supplies to John's army while he maneuvered about Anjou.[27] One is forced to consider the possibility that Peter offered the English king a free passage over the Loire if he would leave Brittany alone for the rest of the campaign. Be that as it may, once he was north of the Loire, John moved on Angers and then settled down to the siege of La Roche-au-Moine.[28]

Peter had maneuvered perfectly. By holding Nantes he had demonstrated his loyalty to King Philip. At the same time by failing to follow John up the Loire to dispute his passage at Oudon or Ancenis he had avoided seriously offending that monarch by permanently blocking his plan of campaign. In the end John's cause was ruined by Peter's wife's uncle, Aimery of Thouars, and his fellow Poitevins. When Prince Louis advanced from Chinon to relieve La Roche-au-Moine, they refused to give battle.[29] To besiege a castle belonging to the seneschal of Anjou was all very well, but a pitched battle with a force led by the heir to the French throne in person was a far more serious matter. The Poitevins, like Peter, had no intention of becoming too deeply compromised before the eventual result of the war was clear. King Philip's overwhelming victory at Bouvines amply justified their caution. When the victorious monarch finally arrived in Poitou, Peter was able to obtain his

---

[27] *Rot. pat.*, p. 117.

[28] Pocquet du Haut-Jussé in *Les papes et les ducs de Bretagne* (Paris, 1928), I, 58 states that Peter went to the aid of La Roche-au-Moine. He bases this statement on a letter of Pope Innocent IV (Morice, *Preuves*, I, 935-939) which complains that Peter forced the men of Nantes to go to the siege of La Roche-sur-Yon. As we know of no siege of the latter place, he concludes that the papal letter intended La Roche-au-Moine. But the letter seems to refer to an event which took place after 1230. To substitute La Roche-au-Moine for La Roche-sur-Yon seems to me to be taking an unjustified liberty with a document.

[29] Wendover, II, 105. Guillaume le Breton, *Philippidos, Oeuvres*, II, 291.

grace for Aimery of Thouars.[30]   John was forced to make a five-year truce.   The duke of Brittany was in good standing with Philip Augustus, and the fact that less than a year later John offered him the honor of Richmond in return for service in England indicates that he had not seriously offended the English monarch.

The battle of Bouvines had frustrated John's plans for recovering his lost continental possessions, but it had not ended the struggle between Plantagenet and Capetian.   The English monarch's quarrels with his barons were soon to give Philip and his son a chance to attempt the conquest of England.   Through the years 1215, 1216, and 1217 Peter worked skillfully and cynically toward his natural goal—the possession of the honor of Richmond.   In August 1215 when John was mustering all his resources to renew the contest which the granting of *Magna Carta* had halted temporarily, he sought aid from Peter.   The duke was offered the honor of Richmond if he would join John with a force of well-equipped knights.[31]   Peter must have been sorely tempted.   King Philip could not with propriety object to his doing homage to John for Richmond and serving him against his rebellious barons.   France and England were at truce, and other barons, notably the great William Marshal, earl of Pembroke and lord of the Norman baronies of Longueville and Orbec, held lands from both sovereigns.   Peter's refusal to accept John's offer was based on more practical reasons than a sense of loyalty to the Capetians.   King John's prospects did not look very good.   His barons were rapidly preparing for civil war, and Louis of France was contemplating going to their assistance.[32]   If the régime in England were to change, it was clearly better to get his fief from the new ruler. Besides there were obvious advantages in winning the favor and gratitude of the heir to the French crown.   By January 1216 Peter had formally enlisted in the army which Prince Louis was gathering for the conquest of England.[33]

[30]Guillaume le Breton, *Gesta, Oeuvres*, I, 298.
[31] *Rot. pat.*, p. 152b.
[32] Petit-Dutaillis, *Louis VIII*, pp. 68-71.
[33] *Littera cuiusdam magnatis* in Roger of Hovedon, *Chronica* (ed. W. Stubbs, *Rolls series*), IV, 189-190.

Louis set sail from Calais on May 20, 1216. With him was Peter's brother, Robert of Dreux, but Peter himself remained behind.[34] In July he attended the court of King Philip at Melun, and he passed August and part of September in Brittany.[35] Sometime toward the end of the latter month he joined Louis in England.[36] While it is possible that Peter's delay was caused by his desire to see how Louis would fare, it is more likely that Philip Augustus was unwilling to lend his son the services of both Robert and Peter. The fact that Robert of Dreux returned to France when his brother arrived in England tends to support this hypothesis.[37] As soon as the young duke joined the host, Louis invested him with the honor of Richmond.[38] This can have been little more than a pleasant gesture —a hope for future reward. The castle and Yorkshire lands of the barony were firmly held by that staunchest of loyalists Earl Ranulf of Chester to whom John had entrusted them as compensation for his lost Norman possessions, and the confusion arising from the war must have made it virtually impossible to collect the revenues of the demesnes in the midland shires. At most Peter may have reaped some profit from the East Anglian lands of the honor. Still, he was in titular possession, and that was something gained.

Soon after Peter's arrival in England the general situation was vitally changed by the sudden death of King John. The deadly foe of the rebel barons was gone, and in his place reigned a young boy. The actual head of the government was the universally trusted and respected William Marshal, earl of Pembroke. Although he was absolutely loyal to the cause of young Henry III, Earl William was a convinced francophile, an old companion in arms of Peter's father, and a vassal of Philip Augustus.[39] He was determined to crush the rebellion and drive the invaders from England, but he was anxious to do

[34] *Histoire des ducs de Normandie*, pp. 165-166.

[35] *Layettes*, I, no. 1182. *Recueil*, nos. 90, 91.

[36] The chronicle of the canon of Barnwell in Walter of Coventry, *Memoriale* (ed. W. Stubbs, *Rolls series*), II, 233. *Histoire des ducs de Normandie*, p. 179.

[37] *Ibid.*

[38] Barnwell, p. 233.

[39] Sidney Painter, *William Marshal* (Baltimore, 1933), pp. 139-140, 254-255.

it as amiably as possible. Early in the spring of 1217 Louis made a truce with the regent and set out for a visit to France.[40] Peter took advantage of the occasion to spend March and part of April in Brittany where he devoted himself to repairing his spiritual fences. The supporters of Louis had all been excommunicated for their temerity in invading a fief held of the pope, and Peter, although his life was passed in fierce quarrels with the church, always kept a wary eye on his spiritual ledger. A pilgrimage to Mont-Saint-Michel and gifts to several monastic houses might balance his activities in England.[41] Late in April he returned to England with Louis.[42]

On May 20, 1217, the crushing defeat of a Franco-baronial army at Lincoln ended Louis' hopes of conquering England. When the victorious regent advanced on London, the French prince sent Peter and the count of Nevers to open negotiations with him.[43] While Peter's mission was to pave the way for the abortive peace conference which took place a few days later, he probably took advantage of the opportunity to discuss his own affairs with the regent. As Louis was not going to be king of England, his grant of the honor of Richmond would be of no value. The obvious course was to see what could be obtained from Earl William. Since the regent was extremely anxious to conclude peace quickly, it was to his interest to gain a friend in Louis' council. As a result he and Peter came to an agreement. Their close relations were shown by the fact that when the final treaty of peace was made, Peter appeared as a guarantor for the payment of the indemnity which was promised to Louis.[44] Late in September the duke of Brittany left England with the French prince, but in the following May he returned to conclude his negotiations with the regent.[45] Earl William made as liberal a settlement as his limited powers would permit. The castle and castellary of Richmond in York-

[40] *Ibid.*, pp. 210, 225-226.

[41] *Recueil*, no. 93. J. Levron, "Catalogue des actes de Pierre de Dreux, duc de Bretagne," *Mémoires de la société d'histoire et d'archéologie de Bretagne,* XI (1930), no. 36. This work will be referred to as Levron, *Catalogue.*

[42] *Histoire des ducs de Normandie,* p. 188.

[43] *Patent rolls, 1216-1225,* p. 68.

[44] *Ibid.*, p. 114.   [45] *Ibid.*, p. 174.

shire had been entrusted by King John to Earl Ranulf of Chester as compensation for the latter's fiefs in Normandy which had been confiscated by Philip Augustus.[46] Even if Earl William had not doubted his authority to terminate grants in custody which had been made by the late king, it would have been out of the question to attempt to dispossess as powerful a baron as Earl Ranulf. Futhermore the regent felt unable to make any arrangements which would commit Henry III when he came of age. He agreed to give Peter provisional possession of all the demesnes of the honor of Richmond outside Yorkshire and the service of all but thirty of the knights' fees.[47] This gave the duke some hundred knights' fees and a number of rich demesne manors including Boston with its extremely valuable fair. While from the point of view of territorial power in England the compact castellary of Richmond with its great castle was the most important part of the honor, the lands below the Humber probably returned a much larger revenue. As Peter was far more interested in cash than in English feudal politics, he did very well in his bargain. For the next six years he was to enjoy a good income from England while continuing in favor at the French court. Peter's use of the title earl of Richmond was no longer merely an empty claim.

Brittany Feels a New Broom

While Peter was skillfully threading his way through the maze of Capetian-Plantagenet relations toward the acquisition of the honor of Richmond, he was also seeking to become master in his own duchy. As titular chief of one of the major fiefs held of the French king, the duke of Brittany was an important figure in the politics of western Europe, but he was not in reality a very potent feudal prince. Brittany was divided into seven counties, and the early feudal dukes had been little more than counts paramount. As time went on, however, they had improved their position. When Geoffrey Plantagenet, third son of Henry II of England, acquired the duchy through

[46] *Rot. pat.*, p. 51.
[47] *Rot. claus.*, I. 385b.

his marriage to Constance, sole heiress of Duke Conan IV, he found himself count of Rennes, Nantes, Vannes, and Quimper —that is, direct lord of all Brittany except for the north coast west of the river Rance. The county of Léon, which occupied the entire northwestern part of the duchy from Lannion to Point St. Mathieu, was held by its ancient comtal dynasty, while the region between Lannion and the Rance which composed the counties of Tréguier and Lamballe was ruled by two branches of a junior line of the ducal house.[48] Backed by the power of Henry II Duke Geoffrey ruthlessly extended his authority. The county of Léon was despoiled of its eastern section, the region about Morlaix, and divided between two brothers. The counts of Lamballe and Tréguier were ejected from their lands. But after Geoffrey's death Count Alan of Tréguier and Count Geoffrey of Lamballe recovered their possessions.[49] When the latter died without heirs of his body in 1205, he left his lands to Count Alan. The feeble Guy of Thouars, who then ruled Brittany as guardian of his daughter Alix, protested against this augmentation of the power of his most dangerous vassal and even went to war with Count Alan. The betrothal of the Duchess Alix to Henry, Count Alan's eldest son, was arranged by King Philip in order to end this dispute and to reward the house of Tréguier for its loyal service to the French crown.[50] When circumstances forced the king to substitute Peter of Dreux for Henry as Alix's fiancé, he did his best to protect the latter's position. Philip promised to see that young Henry enjoyed until he came of age all the lands and privileges which Count Alan had held at his death. He also confirmed Count Alan's appointment of his brother-in-law, Conan of Léon, as guardian of Henry and his lands.[51] Hence when Peter became duke of Brittany, he found the counties of

[48] Arthur de la Borderie, "Nouveau recueil d'actes inédits des ducs de Bretagne et de leur gouvernement," *Mémoires de la société archéologique d'Ille et Vilaine,* XXI (1892), 104, 106-107. This work was published separately at Rennes in 1902. It will be referred to as *Nouveau recueil.*

[49] *Ibid.,* pp. 102-103, 119-120. La Borderie, *Histoire de Bretagne,* II, 54-55, 81-82.

[50] *Nouveau recueil,* p. 108. Morice, *Preuves,* I, 812-813.

[51] L. Delisle, *Catalogue des actes de Philippe-Auguste* (Paris, 1856), nos. 1413, 1414.

Léon, Tréguier, and Lamballe in other hands. Except for the Morlaix district which Duke Geoffrey had seized from the house of Léon, the duke had only a vague suzerainty over the north coast of Brittany.

The great comtal families were not the only reins on the authority of the duke. Even within the counties which he ruled directly his powers were very limited. The ducal demesnes were not extensive.[52] Under Duke Geoffrey they had included the forest of Rennes and the castellany of Ploërmel in the county of Rennes, the Guérande, Gâvre, and Toufou districts in that of Nantes, and a fair part of the southern littoral in those of Vannes and Quimper, but when Philip Augustus had temporarily occupied the duchy in 1206, he had alienated Ploërmel and the Guérande.[53] Even more serious than the poverty of the ducal demesne were the extreme limitations which Breton custom placed on the duke's authority over his barons. The barons of Brittany claimed the right to dispose of the guardianship of their heirs by testament and denied that an heir on coming into his inheritance owed a relief to the duke. Thus the suzerain of Brittany lacked the highly lucrative rights of wardship and relief which were enjoyed by many feudal potentates of the day. The privilege of collecting the revenues which came from wrecked vessels was also claimed by the barons. The long and dangerous coastline of Brittany made this a most valuable feudal perquisite. Finally the duke could neither control the number of castles built by his barons nor exact an oath of fidelity from their vassals.[54] Compared to the duke of Normandy or the count of Champagne the duke of Brittany was a very feeble suzerain. While the Capetian kings and their barons had been extending their power at the expense of their vassals and thus building up powerful feudal states, the weakness of its dukes had left Brittany far behind.

[52] I follow the *Concise Oxford Dictionary* in using the form "demesne" for the technical feudal term *dominium*.

[53] La Borderie, *Histoire de Bretagne*, III, 54-91 and map. *Recueil*, no. 73. *Nouveau recueil*, p. 144, note 1.

[54] *Communes petitiones Britonum et inquisitio facta super eisdem apud S. Briocum et alibi, Nouveau recueil*, pp. 97-102. This document contains the results of an inquest into Peter's treatment of his vassals which was held by order of King Louis IX in 1235.

The same situation existed in respect to the temporal authority of the Breton bishops. While the king seems to have recognized that the local counts had regalian rights over the sees within their lands, this was disputed by several of the prelates. The bishop of Nantes denied that the duke as count of Nantes had these privileges in his see and also claimed to be joint temporal lord of the city of Nantes. Each bishop had a more or less extensive fief, and some claimed absolute authority over their episcopal cities.[55] The bishops of St. Brieuc, Tréguier, and St. Pol depended on the counts of Lamballe, Tréguier, and Léon and thus escaped the duke's control entirely.[56] To the young duke fresh from the atmosphere of King Philip's court the whole governmental system of Brittany must have seemed hopelessly antiquated. He resolved to apply in his duchy the same political methods which Philip had used so successfully in France as a whole. Perhaps the king would appreciate the compliment enough to be willing to overlook Peter's clear violation of his promise not to despoil his barons of lands or privileges which they had previously enjoyed.

Peter lost no time in pitting his conception of the ducal authority against that established by Breton custom. He forbade his barons to build unauthorized castles or to strengthen without his leave those already built. He exacted oaths of fidelity from the vassals of his barons. He also insisted that the enjoyment of the revenues from vessels wrecked on the coast was a ducal prerogative.[57] This last innovation bore with exceptional weight on the counts of Lamballe and Léon who ruled about half the coastline of the duchy. A count of Léon was said to have boasted that he possessed the most precious of all precious stones—a rock on the coast that brought him £5,000 a year in wrecked ships.[58] All these new customs instituted by Peter

[55] For a full discussion of the relations between the dukes and the Breton church see Haut-Jussé, Les papes et les ducs de Bretagne.

[56] Nouveau recueil, pp. 103, 107.

[57] Ibid., pp. 97-102. This information is based on the complaints presented before the royal inquest of 1235.

[58] Ibid., p. 102. The sum is given as 100,000 solidi. The only Breton money which I have been able to evaluate in terms of better known currencies is that of Guingamp. It was worth slightly less than that of Tours. L. Delisle, "Des

were fiercely resented by his barons, but not until he turned to outright seizure of their lands and castles did they venture to resort to open revolt.

While the enforcement of his conception of his rights as a suzerain was a vital part of Peter's policy, his real power in Brittany would depend on his ability to enlarge and enrich the ducal demesne. Castles, cash revenue, and direct vassals formed the bases for the authority of every feudal prince. Hence it was natural that the duke's eyes should turn toward the rich heritage of the house of Tréguier. Young Henry of Tréguier's title to his broad lands was open to question. Precedent was the strongest law known in the Middle Ages, and every duke of Brittany who had been powerful enough had despoiled the counts of Tréguier of a large part of their possessions. Each of Henry's ancestors had held the county, but he could hardly claim that their title had not been disputed by the dukes.[59] His right to the county of Lamballe was still more doubtful. The cession of that region by Count Geoffrey to Alan of Tréguier was a most peculiar proceeding. According to ordinary feudal custom when a vassal died without heirs of his body, the fief either passed to a collateral heir or escheated to the lord. Both Count Geoffrey's sister and the Duchess Alix had a better hereditary claim to Lamballe than Count Alan, and Alix was the suzerain of the fief.[60] Peter could advance a plausible claim to the county either as his wife's inheritance or as a ducal escheat. Count Alan himself had felt little confidence in the validity of his title and had sought to make his position secure through an alliance with King Philip. The king had confirmed the cession of Lamballe and had forced Guy of Thouars to agree to it.[61] At Count Alan's death he had guaranteed young

revenues publics en Normandie au douzième siècle," *Bibliothèque de l'école des chartes*, series II, vol. V (1848-1849), pp. 187, 205. As the return from wrecks on a single rock this figure of £5000 is, of course, ridiculous. It seems unlikely that the count of Léon's entire revenue from wrecks amounted to such a sum. The count was not spoiling his story.

[59] *Nouveau recueil*, no. 4, especially pp. 119-120. This document reports an inquest held in 1235 into the injuries inflicted by the dukes on the house of Tréguier.

[60] See genealogical table no. 2.

[61] *Nouveau recueil*, pp. 116-120.

Henry's enjoyment of his lands until he came of age.[62]   But Philip was far from Brittany, and Henry could only rely on Peter's regard for his promises and the sword of his guardian, Conan of Léon.

Peter cared nothing for his promises to King Philip, and he probably welcomed a war with Conan of Léon. Within thirteen months of his assumption of the ducal title he had gained possession of the county of Lamballe, and by September 1216 he had occupied Lesneven which was Conan's chief seat.[63] Driven from their lands and castles, Conan and his brother, Solomon, waged for six years a fierce guerrilla war against the duke. They were actively supported by many of the vassals of Henry of Tréguier and by the greatest lord of central Brittany, Geoffrey, viscount of Rohan.[64] This pleasant little civil war was complicated in 1221 by the appearance of a new participant. When he was holding Brittany in his own hand in 1206, Philip Augustus had given the important ducal demesne of Ploërmel with its castle to Amaury of Craon, a powerful Angevin baron.[65] This highly questionable grant was ignored by Peter. He seized Ploërmel and expressed his willingness to justify his action before the royal court. Amaury, however, seeing the duke in difficulties with his vassals, preferred a decision by the sword. Being himself a noted warrior, he easily gathered a large army consisting of his own knights, his friends and relatives, and a large contingent of hired mercenaries. Among his auxiliaries were the count of Vendôme and the Angevin baron Hardouin of Maillé. While Peter was fully occupied by his war in the far west, Amaury invaded eastern Brittany and occupied the castles of La Guerche and Châteaubriant.[66]

This invasion of the duchy changed the character of the war in the eyes of the men of Brittany. In a private feud between their duke and some of his vassals they might remain neutral or even aid the rebels, but an attack on Brittany by French

[62] Delisle, *Catalogue des actes de Philippe-Auguste,* no. 1414.
[63] Morice, *Preuves,* I, 822-824. *Recueil,* nos. 86, 87, 91.
[64] Guillaume le Breton, *Philippidos, Oeuvres,* II, 362-363.
[65] *Nouveau recueil,* p. 144 note 1.
[66] Guillaume le Breton, *Philippidos, Oeuvres,* II, 362-363. *Chronicon Sancti Martini Turonensis, Historiens de France,* XVIII, 303.

barons was a different matter. Peter had already bought the
alliance of the viscount of Rohan.[67] Now with the exception
of the lords of Léon who were irreconcilable the Bretons rallied
about their duke. Leaving the house of Léon to plunder at
will in the west, Peter moved against the invader, and on
March 3, 1223, the two armies met before the walls of Châteaubriant. Peter won an overwhelming victory and captured his
chief opponents. Amaury and the count of Vendôme were
consigned to the ducal castle of Toufou until they should
arrange for their ransoms. Not only did the duke force Amaury
to pay a large ransom in money and horses, but he also obliged
him to affiance his eldest daughter to Peter's second son, Arthur,
and to renounce formally his claim to Ploërmel.[68]

The victory of Châteaubriant left Peter undisputed master of
Brittany. For the next eight years no baron of the duchy ven-
tured to risk his anger. The duke remained in full possession
of the county of Lamballe and half that of Tréguier, while
young Henry, who had assumed the surname of Avagor from
one of his demesnes, was reduced to the lordship of the district of Goëllo.[69] As for the lords of Léon, when they learned
of the defeat of their allies, they fled the duchy, but they soon
returned to come to terms with the duke. By 1225 Conan and
his kinsmen were in attendance at Peter's court.[70] In addition
to conquering lands and castles, the duke gained possession of
the regalian rights over the sees of St. Brieuc, Tréguier, and St.

[67] Morice, Preuves, I, 846.

[68] Guillaume le Breton, Philippidos, Oeuvres, II, 364. Chronicon Sancti
Martini Turonensis, Historiens de France, XVIII, 303. Nouveau recueil, no. 14.
It is impossible to establish a satisfactory chronology for the war between
Peter and his barons. The occupation of Lamballe and Lesneven indicate the
beginning in 1214-1216 while the battle of Châteaubriant marks the end in
March 1223. If Peter's decision to buy peace with the viscount of Rohan and
the bishop of Nantes marked the start of Amaury's invasion, that took place in
the summer of 1221. Morice, Preuves, I, 846. It is, however, hard to believe
that Amaury spent a year and a half in Brittany. Perhaps his preparations were
extended over some time. The whole problem seems insoluble.

[69] Nouveau recueil, pp. 106-121, especially pp. 114-115.

[70] Guillaume le Breton, Philippidos, Oeuvres, II, 364-365. Morice, Preuves,
I, 853-855.

Pol.[71] There were no longer counts of Léon, Tréguier, and Lamballe—Conan and Hervé of Léon and Henry of Avagor were simply barons of Brittany. Peter had crushed his most dangerous vassals and succeeded in establishing in Brittany the feudal usages to which he had been accustomed in France. At the same time he had increased the ducal demesnes by lands worth £4,000 of Tours a year.[72]

The same determination to augment the ducal authority which brought on the war with his barons led Peter into conflict with the church in the person of the bishop of Nantes. The city of Nantes was the richest and most prosperous town of Brittany. It was the depot for the commerce of the Loire—especially the lucrative wine trade with England—and the center for the sale of the salt which was manufactured in the extensive marshes of the region about. What revenue the duke was to draw from commerce must come largely from Nantes. But the bishop claimed joint sovereignty over the city and denied that the duke could impose new taxes without his consent.[73] The questions at issue were purely temporal. The bishop of Nantes was a baron who claimed privileges which were incompatible with Peter's conception of the duke's prerogative.

During the years 1216 and 1217 the duke was in continual need of money for his English ventures, and his eye turned naturally toward the possibilities offered by the commerce of Nantes. His first step was to establish monopolies by decree. Wood sold must come from his forests, salt from his works, flour from his mills. This, of course, was a serious blow to the bishop who also owned forests, mills, and salt works. It deprived him of a market for his surplus. Then Peter imposed a sales tax on all goods sold. Stephen, bishop of Nantes, protested vigorously and denied the legality of Peter's decrees, but the duke simply ordered his agents to enforce them. He

---

[71] *Nouveau recueil*, pp. 103, 106-107.

[72] This is Henry of Avagor's estimate of the annual value of the Breton lands taken from him by Peter. *Querimonia Henrici de Avaugor, anno 1247, Historiens de France*, XXIV, 729-731.

[73] Morice, *Preuves*, I, 802-804. Haut-Jussé, *Les papes et les ducs de Bretagne*, I, 57-58.

was obeyed with rather overwhelming enthusiasm. His officers plundered the lands of the bishop, his clergy, and his vassals and burned their houses. They even seized members of the clergy and forced them to ransom themselves.[74] The duke clearly intended to teach the bishop the disadvantages of resistance to his will.

The bishop excommunicated the duke and appealed to Rome. Honorius III in letters of April 20, 1218, appointed a commission of strict churchmen headed by the bishop of Le Mans to investigate the case and take appropriate action.[75] But Peter had not been taken by surprise. His own envoys arrived in Rome soon after those sent by the bishop and argued his cause so successfully that Honorius appointed a new commission, composed exclusively of Breton clergy, to free the duke from excommunication pending settlement of the dispute.[76] Meanwhile Bishop Stephen, finding his position untenable, had placed an interdict on the ducal demesnes in his diocese and then fled the duchy and sought refuge at Tours.[77] On June 28, 1219, Honorius came to his support with letters ordering the bishop of La Mans' commission to publish the excommunication of Peter in the whole province of Tours and to lay an interdict on all Brittany.[78] On July 31 he wrote to Peter threatening papal confirmation of the excommunication and the release of his vassals from their oaths of fidelity.[79] On December 7 the pope ordered the archbishops of Sens, Tours, Bourges, and Rouen to launch the papal excommunication.[80]

While Peter waged relentless war on the church of Nantes and defied Christ's vicar by joining Louis' invasion of England, he prudently courted divine favor by benefactions to various ecclesiastical corporations. The abbeys of St. Sulpice and St. Melaine of Rennes, the priory of Combourg depending on Marmoutier, and the order of the Temple were recipients of his bounty.[81] To the Templars his generosity was so great that he

[74] Morice, *Preuves*, I, 835.   [75] *Ibid.*
[76] *Regesta Honorii papae III* (ed. P. Pressuti, Rome, 1888-1895), no. 1550.
[77] *Ibid.*, no. 1501.   [78] *Ibid.*, no. 1482.
[79] *Ibid.*, no. 1561.   [80] *Ibid.*, no. 1725.
[81] *Recueil*, nos. 85, 89, 92. Morice, *Preuves*, I, 836. Levron, *Catalogue*, nos. 21, 42.

won them as faithful allies throughout his turbulent career. But these were comparatively minor weights in the celestial scales—far too slight to counterbalance the solemn papal excommunication. Fortunately in the spring of 1219 an opportunity appeared which might allow Peter to win the favor of both God and His deputy on earth. Louis of France was preparing to lead an army to the aid of Amaury of Montfort who was hard beset by the Albigensian heretics. When the crusading host started south in May, Peter was in its ranks in the hope that brave deeds against the heretics might persuade the pope to lift his excommunication.[82] But this crusade brought little glory either celestial or terrestrial. The army besieged and took the little town of Marmande, but retired from the defiant walls of Toulouse. Peter's sole recorded exploit was the preservation of the life of the count of Astarac, commander of the forces in Marmande, from the ardor of the bishops. At the insistence of the duke and his cousin the count of St. Pol the noble prisoners were spared, even though all of lesser rank were put to the sword.[83] By December Peter was back in Nantes still excommunicate.[84]

Meanwhile the bishop of Nantes had gone to Rome to plead his cause in person. There he met Peter's agents. Under the guidance of the Cardinal Thomas of Capua an agreement was drawn up which was a complete victory for the bishop. The duke was to abolish his monopolies and sales taxes. The bishop was to regain his lands and receive all the revenues which the duke's officers had collected from them. He was to enjoy all his ancient privileges. Peter's agents were to pay heavy damages and to suffer corporal penance for their offenses. The duke himself was to pay £500 damages. The papal letters of January 28, 1220, which announced this accord appointed a commission to supervise its execution.[85] But the resourceful duke was not yet defeated. By far the most valuable of the

---

[82] Petit-Dutaillis, *Louis VIII*, pp. 195-197. Pressuti, no. 1981. Guillaume le Breton, *Gesta, Oeuvres*, I, 319.

[83] *Ibid.* *La chanson de la croisade contre les Albigeois* (ed. Paul Meyer, Société de l'histoire de France, Paris, 1875), I, 370-374.

[84] *Recueil*, no. 98.

[85] Morice, *Preuves*, I, 840-841.

monopolies in question and the one most annoying to the bishop was that on salt. If Peter could retain that he would have much. Rome had decided against him—he would turn to Paris where ruled as cheerful and enthusiastic a baiter of the clergy as the age knew. On May 24, 1220, Thierry de Gallardon, seneschal of Touraine and Poitou, held an inquiry as to the respective rights of the bishop and duke over the salt trade at Nantes. King Philip's officer chose his witnesses with care. They included three barons of Brittany, two of Peter's seneschals, and some rich burghers of Nantes whose prosperity depended largely on ducal favor. The only ecclesiastics were an unimportant prior, a Cistercian monk, and the local master of the Templars whose order was devoted to the duke. This neatly packed panel unanimously declared that the duke could regulate the salt trade at his pleasure.[86] The decision was a most useful weapon. It gave Peter an excuse to delay his confirmation of the concord made at Rome while he continued to enjoy the revenue of the see of Nantes. In fact the ingenious duke might have prolonged the controversy indefinitely were it not for other circumstances. When Peter in the midst of his war with the house of Léon learned that Amaury of Craon was planning to invade Brittany, he decided that he had too many enemies. On August 2, 1221, he suddenly made full submission to the bishop of Nantes.[87] Thus the comparatively gentle introduction to his later bitter controversies with his bishops came to an inglorious end.

In considering Peter's quarrels with his barons and clergy one cannot but wonder what the wily and ageing Philip Augustus thought of his young protegé. The duke had cheerfully violated the solemn promises which he had made when doing homage for the duchy. Not only had he ignored his general agreement not to despoil his barons of privileges or possessions without the approval of Philip's court, but he had seized the lands of Henry of Avagor who was definitely under the king's protection. He had even refused to recognize Philip's own charter granting Ploërmel to Amaury of Craon. Why then did

---

[86] *Ibid.*, columns 846-847.

[87] *Ibid.* For a full discussion of this whole controversy see Haut-Jussé, *Les papes et les ducs de Bretagne*, I, 60-71.

the king take no action to protect his friends and force Peter to observe his promises? One cannot, unfortunately, penetrate the fastnesses of King Philip's mind. It is quite possible that when he heard of Peter's activities, the old man smiled indulgently and murmured, " He is a true Capetian," but no chronicler has been kind enough to report the incident. William the Breton, Philip's court historian, does, however, furnish a clue to the king's attitude. In discussing Peter's war with the lords of Léon, William, who seems to have had an acute personal interest in the fortunes of that house, states that there was justice on both sides. While Conan and his kinsmen were justified in defending their inheritance, Peter had every right to attempt to exercise the ducal prerogatives which they had usurped.[88] So fairly balanced a statement from a Breton friendly to the house of Léon indicates strongly that the general opinion of Philip and his court was sympathetic to Peter. But as a matter of fact the king's personal inclinations probably had little to do with his decision. He was a practical man who had the interests of the monarchy in mind. Peter's French fiefs were insignificant. Philip's only effective means of coercing him was a formal military expedition. Even if the king could convince the barons of France that he was justified in interfering in Peter's relations with his vassals, it would not be worth the cost. No direct interests of the monarchy were involved. Count Alan had been a valuable ally of France, but Henry of Avagor was a helpless child. The lords of Léon were far from being noted for their love of the French crown. As for Amaury of Craon, he was already too powerful to suit Philip's taste, and a few reverses to his pride were highly desirable.

Ironically enough the years which witnessed Peter's success in making himself master of the Breton baronage marked the end of his reign as duke. On October 21, 1221, the Duchess Alix died, and her title and lands passed to her eldest son, John of Brittany.[89] While the fact that John was but four years old secured for Peter the actual control of the duchy until his son

[88] Guillaume le Breton, *Philippidos, Oeuvres*, II, 362.
[89] Morice, *Preuves*, I, 107.

came of age, he would rule as custodian rather than as duke.[90] He might still issue acts as duke of Brittany and earl of Richmond, but they would have force only as long as his regency continued. Worse yet, a baron inclined to rebellion could always assert his complete loyalty to the infant duke while defying Peter. The loss of Alix also weakened Peter's position in French politics. The crown's jurisdiction over the guardian of a minor vassal was far greater than over the vassal himself. Although Peter's formal title did not change, the descent from duke to custodian was a very real one.

Little can be said about the personality of the Duchess Alix. As she was only twenty-one when she died, it seems unlikely that she can have had much influence over her headstrong and turbulent spouse who was her senior by ten or eleven years.[91] The fact that Peter's pious benefactions decreased and his quarrels with the church waxed fiercer after her death may indicate that she was able to moderate his anti-clerical tendencies, but again this change may have been a coincidence. Alix bore her husband three children, John, Yolande, and Arthur. John was born in the autumn of either 1216 or 1217.[92] While there is no satisfactory evidence as to the date of birth of either Yolande or Arthur, the youth of their mother makes it probable that they were younger than John. Yolande was almost certainly

[90] In June 1230 the court of Louis IX declared that Peter had forfeited the *ballum Britannie*. The barons of Brittany were said to have done him homage *ratione illius balli*. *Layettes*, II, no. 2056.

[91] The date of Peter's birth is unknown. I base my calculations on the fact that he and his elder brother were knighted in 1209. As it is unlikely that Count Robert II would have delayed the dubbing of his eldest son beyond his twenty-first year, I assume that Peter was no older than nineteen or twenty in 1209. As their parents were married in 1184, it seems improbable that Robert and Peter were younger than this.

[92] The chronicles date his birth in 1217 and 1218. Morice, *Preuves*, I, 107. But he was recognized as of age by Louis IX on November 16, 1237. *Cartulaire de Vitré*, no. 399. In 1230 it had been expressly provided that John should be of age when he reached his twenty-first year. *Layettes*, II, no. 2059. If one uses modern methods of computing age, John must have been born in 1216. It seems likely, however, that he was considered to be twenty-one on his twenty-first birthday and hence born in 1217.

born before 1219.[93] Arthur's name leads one to wonder if he were not born during the most crucial period of Peter's war with his vassals when the duke needed the support of the Celtic Bretons. His birth may well have been the occasion for his mother's death. Arthur died a few years after his betrothal to Isabel of Craon, but John and Yolande survived to play important parts in the life of their day and in their father's biography. Alix had faithfully performed the chief function of feudal womanhood.

Dame Alix would be for us merely a name on a few time-stained charters, the nebulous progenitrix of a noble line of Breton dukes, had she not married a man who while he may well have been a fond husband and devoted father, was certainly an ambitious and arrogant baron. But some fortunate mixture of affection, piety, and pride moved Peter to enshrine his family where he, his wife, and his two elder children would shine forth in varied colors from the lancet windows of the south transept of the cathedral of Chartres to rejoice the eyes of countless generations. In the lower part of the central lancet glow Peter's arms—alternate squares of blue and gold which designated the house of Dreux quartered with ermines which were Peter's personal insignia.[94] The two lancets to the right of the center are occupied by Peter and John, those to the left by Alix and Yolande. Peter, kneeling in prayer in an armorial surcoat, looks far from comfortable and prepared for

[93] She barely escaped being married to Count Thibaut of Champagne in 1231 or 1232. It would have been most unusual to marry a girl under twelve to a mature man. It is quite possible that John and Yolande were twins. This would account for the phraseology of a document of 1230 *salvo iure Johannis ......et Yolandis......quando venerint ad etatem viginti et unius anni. Layettes,* II, no. 2059.

[94] I can find no basis for the generally accepted belief that the ermines represented the arms of Brittany which Peter quartered on the arms of Dreux. L. C. Douet-d'Arcq, *Collection de sceaux* (Paris, 1863-1868), no. 534.   There is no evidence that Guy of Thouars or any earlier duke of Brittany used the ermines as arms. Then the ermines are found on Peter's seal attached to the document of January 29, 1213, which announced his homage to Philip Augustus. *Ibid.,* no. 725. As in the body of this document and on the seal itself Peter is designated as "Peter, son of Count Robert of Dreux and Braine," this seems conclusive proof that he added the ermines to his arms before he married Alix and became duke of Brittany.

instant flight from his pious environment. As the feelings of a Christian martyr must have been very similar to those of Peter in prayer, it would be useless to probe the mind of the artist for his model. Peter looks unhappy—but so do the saints above him. Alix, John, and Yolande with their attending saints seem far more content. But Peter had no intention of letting posterity see him only as the dutiful father of his family. He used a neighboring bay to depict himself mounted in full armor with shield and lance. His great sheathed sword decorated with an armorial pommel stands almost straight out behind him over his horse's back. Perhaps this like the tortured face of the kneeling figure was designed to indicate the restless disposition of the artist's subject.[95]

Peter's monument to his wife and family was conceived on a grand scale. In addition to the rose window with its five lancets at the end of the transept and the windows in the two adjacent bays he gave the magnificent south porch with its exquisite sculptures. There over the head of the central Christ are Peter and Alix feeding the poor.[96] Peter's donation as a whole rivals if it does not actually outshine that of the royal family itself. His gift honors Christ, the King—theirs only His Virgin Mother. The ducal house of Brittany was to reign in the southern sunlight while their Capetian rivals were left on the bleak northern side. Peter's gift to Chartres was conceived on the scale of his ambitions rather than on that of his actual position in the feudal world. One cannot help wondering, however, whether the duke's princely munificence to Chartres was not paid for largely with money extorted from the Breton church. If Peter really made his clergy pay the cost of the celestial glory of the reigning house of Brittany, it was a true masterstroke. In any case, posterity owes him its gratitude for sublime works of art.

[95] A full description of these windows with excellent reproductions will be found in Y. Delaporte and E. Houvet, *Les vitraux de la cathédrale de Chartres* (Chartres, 1926), pp. 429-437; planches 196-204.

[96] E. Houvet, *Monographie de la cathédrale de Chartres*, p. 13.

II

SUCCESSFUL OPPORTUNISM

Duke For Sale

The death of the Duchess Alix wrought a fundamental change in the nature of Peter's ambitions. While his wife lived, he had been content to develop to the fullest possible extent his authority and influence as duke of Brittany. But now his tenure of the ducal dignity had become temporary—in sixteen years he would be obliged to yield his rights over the duchy to his son. Henceforth his principal interest would lie in securing for himself a position of comfort, dignity, and political importance which he could enjoy after John reached his majority. In order to achieve this end Peter had to acquire fiefs which were not part of Alix's inheritance. This purpose was to dominate his policy throughout the years in which he ruled Brittany as regent for his son. Peter became an adventurer who used the resources of his duchy to further his private ambitions. He became a gambler who cheerfully risked the loss of Brittany in schemes to achieve power and wealth for himself. It is, however, important to remember that he was staking nothing more permanent than his right of custody. Nothing Peter might do could affect the position of John of Brittany. Feudal usage provided that when the young duke reached his majority he would enjoy all the lands and privileges which his mother had possessed at her death.

Peter did not have long to wait for opportunities to start on his new path. On July 14, 1223, the aged Philip Augustus died and was succeeded by his son Louis, a vigorous and bellicose prince of thirty-eight. The new king was determined to adopt an aggressive policy. He would either lead another crusade against the Albigensians or attempt to eject the English from Poitou and Gascony.[1] Moreover the accession of Louis was bound to make the English government more belligerent

---

[1] Petit-Dutaillis, *Louis VIII*, pp. 234-238.

toward the French crown. The treaty of Lambeth which terminated Louis' invasion of England had been supplemented by various oral agreements, and the men who ruled in the name of young Henry III were firmly convinced that one of these had provided that when Louis succeeded his father he would return to the Plantagenets the continental fiefs of which Philip had despoiled them. If Louis had really made such a promise, he certainly had no intention of observing it. Hence as soon as it became clear to Henry's advisers that they could not recover the lost provinces by diplomacy, their minds turned to plans for war.[2] This situation was an immense boon to the ambitious and not too scrupulous duke of Brittany. Louis knew that Peter's pleasant annual revenue from the honor of Richmond made him inclined to cherish the favor of the English government and that the strategic location of Brittany made it inevitable that Henry's advisers would be willing to bid high for the support of its duke. Before the king could embark on either of the enterprises which he was contemplating, he would have to secure Peter's fidelity. If Louis neglected to win the alliance of the duke of Brittany by bestowing fiefs on Peter of Dreux, the English would be certain to do so.

After toying for some months with the idea of a crusade, Louis decided early in 1224 to attempt to conquer Poitou and Gascony. The time seemed highly propitious. The justiciar, Hubert de Burgh, who was ruling England for young Henry, was fully occupied by opposition at home and could send little aid to the English officers on the continent. The momentary impotence of the English government made it easy for Louis to secure Peter's full support. The king apparently agreed that in return for assisting in the invasion of Poitou the duke might retain any lands he could conquer from English partisans who dwelt on the Breton marches. Having secured the loyalty of his most dangerous vassal, Louis entered into negotiations with the real master of Poitou, Hugh of Lusignan, count of La Marche and Angoulême. From line after line of strong castles Hugh, his relatives, and his vassals dominated central and southern Poitou. The political position of the count of La

---

[2] *Ibid.*, pp. 175-176, 233. Painter, *William Marshal*, p. 224.

Marche was very similar to that of Peter. By his marriage to Isabel, countess of Angoulême and widow of King John, Hugh was the stepfather of Henry III, and when he was on good terms with his stepson's government, he could enjoy the revenues of his wife's rich English dowry. Hence he had strong reasons for remaining loyal to Henry III. But Hugh was a confirmed intriguer whose allegiance was always for sale. In May 1224 he reached an agreement with King Louis. In return for lands, castles, and revenues Count Hugh promised his aid against his stepson. One clause of the treaty provided that whenever Louis should be in Poitou, the castle of Lusignan should be placed in the care of the duke of Brittany.[3] While this could be taken as an indication that Peter had been instrumental in bringing Louis and Hugh together, it may well have meant simply that he was the sole baron reasonably acceptable to both parties. Be that as it may, the similarity of their policies was bound to serve as a tie between Peter and the count of La Marche. Both were engaged in the delicate game of drawing all possible profit from the struggle between the Capetian and Plantagenet dynasties. Of all the barons who could advance plausible arguments for allegiance to either crown they were by far the most powerful.

The desertion of Hugh of Lusignan made the English position in Poitou essentially hopeless. Louis mustered his host at Tours on June 24, 1224. By July 15 he had taken Niort and St. Jean d'Angéli and had laid siege to La Rochelle. That place, the chief English stronghold in Poitou, capitulated early in August.[4] Nothing is known of Peter's part in this short and successful campaign. Presumably he occupied the castle of Lusignan in accordance with the terms of the treaty between Louis and the count of La Marche. He was certainly present at the fall of La Rochelle.[5] But he had little real interest in the fate of Poitou and Gascony. While Hugh of Lusignan led a royal army toward Bordeaux, Peter hurried northward to collect his reward in the valley of the Loire. On the southern

---

[3] *Veterum scriptorum et monumentorum amplissima collectio* (edd. E. Martène and U. Durand, Paris, 1724-1733), I, 1184-1186.

[4] Petit-Dutaillis, *Louis VIII*, pp. 238-245.

[5] *Ibid.*, pp. 443, 448.

bank of that stream opposite the Breton town of Oudon stood the castle of Champtoceaux which belonged to Thibaut Crespin, an Angevin baron who had remained loyal to the Plantagenets. For years Thibaut had preyed on the commerce of the Loire, and his depredations probably weighed very heavily on Peter's merchants of Nantes. The castle was of considerable strategic importance as it watched both the river and the crossing to Oudon. Furthermore, Thibaut possessed another stronghold, Montfaucon, which stood in the extreme southwestern corner of Anjou only a few miles from the Breton border fortress of Clisson. Its possession would not only add a strong castle to the all too feeble line which covered Brittany from the south, but it would also give Peter an excellent base for military activities in northern Poitou. As soon as he reached home after the fall of La Rochelle, the duke laid siege to Champtoceaux. Thibaut defended it vigorously, but eventually Peter's siege engines forced him to surrender. Thibaut was despoiled of his lands and driven into exile.[6] In October King Louis formally granted Peter as a fief the castles of Champtoceaux and Montfaucon with all the lands of Thibaut Crespin. As he realized that this might simply replace one robber baron by another, the king required Peter to swear that he would refrain from plundering the commerce of the Loire.[7] Since these acquisitions were not part of Brittany, they would remain in Peter's possession after he lost the duchy. Thus the campaign of 1224 yielded the first installment of his old age pension.

Peter must have realized that his part in the invasion of Poitou and his attack on Thibaut Crespin were likely to lead to the loss of his English possessions, but he probably believed that the deprivation would be a temporary one. If Henry III was to save any of his continental lands, he needed every friend he could find, and the duke of Brittany was far too important a baron to alienate permanently. As a matter of fact the English government seemed inclined to overlook Peter's participation in the Poitevin campaign. It was only when Thibaut Crespin appeared in England to seek redress for his injuries

[6] *Chronicon Sancti Martini Turonensis, Historiens de France,* XVIII, 305-306.
[7] Morice, *Preuves,* I, 852.

that the regency felt obliged to act. On November 3 Peter's English lands were placed in the custody of Thomas de Moulton, and Thibaut received a pension from the English king.[8] But early in the spring of 1225 Henry's counselors opened fresh negotiations not only with Peter but also with his brother Count Robert III of Dreux.[9] Robert had married the heiress of Thomas of St. Valéry and thus acquired a claim to the English barony held by that house. The two brothers were eager to negotiate. By March 8 Count Robert's chaplain was in England, and safe-conducts were issued for Robert and Peter.[10] There is no clear proof that they took advantage of these letters to visit England, but in all probability they did. At any rate, either in person or through emissaries they came to an agreement with the English government. Peter recovered all the lands which he had held since 1219. Count Robert seems to have been given a pension of £166 a year in lieu of actual possession of the honor of St. Valéry. As for Thibaut Crespin the regency salved its conscience by formally ordering Peter to return his lands and castles.[11] Needless to say this command was cheerfully ignored. Peter had eaten his cake with relish and yet still had it safely in hand.

The acquisition of a minor Angevin barony was not, however, enough to satisfy Peter's ambition. He was a great baron of France and wished to remain one after his son came of age. Only by marrying another rich heiress could he secure his future position. With this end in view the duke's fertile mind devised a masterstroke. Jeanne, countess of Flanders, had apparently never been very compatible with her husband Ferrand of Portugal, and now he had lain for over eleven years in a French prison.[12] Both Philip Augustus and Louis had turned deaf ears toward every plea for Ferrand's release. In the spring of 1224 Louis had ignored a particularly fervent supplication ad-

[8] *Rot. claus.*, II, 4, 12b. *Calendar of liberate rolls, 1226-1240* (*Rolls series*), pp. 39, 43, 89, 293. *Patent rolls, 1225-1232*, p. 314.

[9] *Rot. claus.*, II, 36.

[10] *Ibid.*, p. 22. *Patent rolls, 1216-1225*, p. 512.

[11] *Rot. claus.*, II, 26b, 28b, 36, 72.

[12] Le Nain de Tillemont, *Vie de Saint Louis roi de France* (ed. J. de Gaulle, Société de l'histoire de France, Paris, 1847), I, 448-449.

dressed to him by Honorius III and his cardinals.[13] Flanders needed the rule of a strong hand, and the countess was in perpetual difficulty. She would be glad to acquire a husband who could defend her rights at home and abroad. If Peter could persuade the pope to annul Jeanne's marriage to Ferrand, the rich heiress he needed would be in his grasp—unless Louis VIII objected too violently.

The duke dispatched emissaries to Rome to plead his and Jeanne's cause before Honorius and then set to work to make certain of the benevolence of King Louis.[14] That monarch had again turned his eyes toward the Midi. If he was to lead his host against the Albigensians, it was absolutely essential that he be assured of the loyalty of those of his vassals who were in a position to intrigue with England. Peter was in Paris in January 1226 when the crusade was being planned, and his name stands second to that of the king's half-brother, Count Philip of Boulogne, in the baronial manifesto which urged Louis to undertake an expedition against the heretics.[15] The duke's cultivation of Louis' favor was reasonably successful. When William, bishop of Chalons and count of Perche, died in February 1226, the king entrusted to Peter's custody the castles of Bellême and La Perrière with their appurtenances. He also gave him the custody of the stronghold of St. James which stood on the river Beuvron in the marches between Brittany and Normandy.[16] While the grant of part of the county of Perche was purely gratuitous, Peter had some claim to St. James. Under the Plantagenets the hereditary constableship of this castle had belonged to the earls of Chester. When King John entrusted Richmond castle to Ranulf of Chester, Philip Augustus gave St. James to Guy of Thouars.[17] Hence Peter may well have felt that he was entitled to the custody of this stronghold as long as Earl Ranulf held Richmond. Neverthe-

[13] *Layettes*, II, nos. 1644, 1645.

[14] *Chronicon Sancti Martini Turonensis, Historiens de France*, XVIII, 316.

[15] *Layettes*, II, no. 1742.

[16] Guillaume de Nangis, *Gesta Ludovici regis, Historiens de France*, XX, 312.

[17] F. M. Powicke, *The loss of Normandy* (Manchester, 1913), p. 115. L. Delisle, *Cartulaire Normand* (Caen, 1852), nos. 140, 141.

less these two concessions demonstrated King Louis' anxiety to secure Peter's loyalty.

Peter's agents in Rome appear to have succeeded in obtaining papal letters annulling the marriage of Ferrand and Jeanne.[18]   As the duke of Brittany was hardly noted for his devotion to the church, one may suspect that Honorius hoped to force Louis to release Ferrand by presenting the king with an alternative which was still more unpleasant. If such was the papal strategy, it worked perfectly. The county of Flanders was from the king's point of view a particularly undesirable location for Peter. Not only was it extremely exposed to English influence, but it was also adjacent to the part of France where Peter's relatives were most numerous and powerful. Peter still had eleven years to rule as duke of Brittany. King Louis could hardly view with equanimity the prospect of having the royal demesne flanked on both the north and the west by the lands of this ambitious and unscrupulous baron. When Louis learned of the papal letters of annullment, he acted promptly. In April 1226 he issued a formal promise to free Count Ferrand by Christmas and required the Countess Jeanne to swear that she would remarry him at once.[19]

The king's action enraged Peter. He was Louis' relative and had been as loyal as a duke of Brittany could be expected to be. Ladies whose hands carried with them the enjoyment of major fiefs were extremely rare, and Peter was unlikely to find another opportunity for a really profitable marriage. Up to this time Peter had been simply a grasping baron whose political interests were not always those of the crown. The king's disruption of his plan to marry Jeanne of Flanders not only forced him to consider other means of providing for his future, but also made him inclined to turn toward the enemies of the monarch who had so gravely affronted him. His first move was to enter into negotiations with Richard Plantagenet, earl of Cornwall and count of Poitou, who was in nominal com-

[18] These letters have never been found. The *Chronicle of Tours*, however, states that Peter obtained them. *Chronicon Sancti Martini Turonensis, Historiens de France*, XVIII, 316. The issuance of the letters is also indicated by the fact that Louis obliged Jeanne to remarry Ferrand. *Layettes*, II, no. 1763.

[19] *Ibid.*, nos. 1761-1763.

mand in Gascony for his brother King Henry III. Peter and
the counselors of the sixteen-year-old English prince seem to
have concocted a scheme for the marriage of Earl Richard to
Peter's daughter Yolande as the basis for a close alliance between England and Brittany.[20] Then the duke began to sound
out his fellow vassals of the French crown. His plan was to
form a baronial league which would act in concert with England. In this way Peter hoped to humble King Louis and win
for himself by force of arms generous compensation for the
loss of Jeanne of Flanders.

Two barons of France lent willing ears to the suggestions
of the duke of Brittany. Thibaut, count palatine of Champagne and Brie, was a sensitive, mercurial young man with a
decided talent for the composition of lyric poetry. Although
in general Thibaut was volatile in affection and purpose, his
life knew at least two enduring emotions. He had a profound
dislike for Louis VIII and a romantic admiration for the latter's
wife, Blanche of Castille. Contemporary scandal-mongers believed that the count's lust for the queen made him hate the
king whose existence made his desires hopeless.[21] While this
may be true, there is no need to assume that Thibaut burned
with passion for Blanche in order to explain his enmity toward
Louis. Thibaut had been a posthumous child and had passed
the first twenty-one years of his reign under the guardianship
of his mother, Blanche of Navarre. Life was never pleasant
for a woman and child at the head of a great fief. Finding
herself surrounded by enemies who threatened her son's inheritance, the Countess Blanche sought the aid of her suzerain,

[20] The fact that Peter opened negotiations with Richard is attested by a letter
written by Henry III to the pope. *Close rolls, 1234-1237*, pp. 169-170. The
plan to marry Yolande to Richard is mentioned only in Philippe Mousket,
Chronique rimée (ed. Reiffenberg, *Collection de chroniques Belges inédites*,
Brussels, 1838), II, 563. As Yolande was affianced to Henry III in October
1226 (*Patent rolls, 1225-1232*, pp. 153-154), it is quite possible that Mousket
confused the brothers and that there was no idea of marrying Richard and
Yolande. See L. A. Vigneras, " Sur une poesie de Thibaut de Navarre," *Modern
language notes*, XLVIII (1933), 336-338 and S. Painter, " The historical setting
of *Robert veez de Perron*," *ibid.*, LII (1937), 83-87.

[21] Petit-Dutaillis, *Louis VIII*, p. 323. Élie Berger, *Histoire de Blanche de
Castille, reine de France* (Paris, 1895), p. 83. Wendover, II, 313.

Philip Augustus. That practical minded monarch exacted a high price in cash and political concessions in return for nothing more potent than moral support. Blanche of Navarre saved the fief for her son, but she was forced to buy off her foes at a ruinous price.[22] Throughout this affair Louis of France had cooperated fully with his father. Then in 1219 Thibaut had planned to lead a crusade against the Albigensians and had secured the pope's approval, but Philip intervened and gave the command of the expedition to Louis.[23] There was reason enough why this young noble, scion of the proudest feudal house of France, should hate the Capetian king and enter into the schemes of Peter of Dreux. The other malcontent whom Peter won to his cause was that perpetual intriguer, Hugh of Lusignan. He had been bought by Louis in 1224 and was beginning to wonder what Henry III would pay to regain his allegiance. His most cherished ambition was to possess the great town of Bordeaux. Louis had failed to conquer it for him—Henry had it to give. Sometime during the summer of 1226 Peter, Thibaut, and Hugh entered into an alliance against " all men or creatures who can be born, live, or die." There was no need to mention Louis specifically. The fact that the treaty of alliance contained no reservation safeguarding the rights of their common suzerain made it sufficiently clear against whom the league was directed.[24]

Meanwhile, in May 1226 King Louis had mustered his crusading army at Bourges, and early in June he settled down to the siege of Avignon. Peter and his fellow conspirator, Thibaut of Champagne, were careful to avoid a technical default in their feudal obligations. Count Thibaut joined Louis soon after the investment of Avignon, and Peter apparently arrived some-

[22] For a full account of the regency of Blanche of Navarre see H. D'Arbois de Jubainville, *Histoire des ducs et des comtes de Champagne* (Paris, 1861-1865), IV.

[23] *Ibid.*, V, no. 1189 ter. This reference is to the catalogue of acts attached to Jubainville. It will be referred to as Jubainville, *Catalogue*. See also Petit-Dutaillis, *Louis VIII*, pp. 88-89, 204-205, 323.

[24] Morice, *Preuves*, I, 856-857. Dated simply 1226 these documents could have been drawn up at any time between Easter 1226 and mid-February 1227, but it is clear that Peter and Hugh at least were allies by October 1226. *Patent rolls, 1225-1232*, pp. 153-154.

what later.[25] Neither of these barons was any asset to the army. The *Chronicle of Tours* blames their treason for the repulse of an assault which cost the life of Count Guy of St. Pol. Count Thibaut openly favored the count of Toulouse and the inhabitants of the besieged city. Soon after the completion of the forty days service that was required by feudal custom, he withdrew from the host and returned to Champagne.[26] The fact that Peter did not share the general opprobrium which Thibaut suffered for this desertion of his liege lord indicates that the duke remained with Louis until the fall of Avignon in September.

Daughter Twice Sold

The crusade had merely momentarily suspended Peter's negotiations with England. Early in the autumn the tentative arrangements made between the duke and Richard of Cornwall were considered by Henry III and his advisers. One important change was made in the plan—Henry himself replaced his brother as Yolande's fiancé. On October 19, 1226, a formal treaty was concluded. Henry III was to marry Yolande of Brittany as soon as the pope's permission could be obtained. The marriage required a papal dispensation because Henry and Yolande were within the prohibited degrees of kinship.[27] Once wed, Henry would aid the duke " to defend and seek his rights " and would make neither peace nor truce with Peter's enemies without his consent. If this alliance cost the duke his French fiefs, Henry would give him the rest of the honor of Richmond

[25] Petit-Dutaillis, *Louis VIII*, p. 323. Thibaut signed a letter sent by the barons of the host to Frederick II. *Layettes*, II, no. 1789. As Peter's name does not appear, I assume that he had not yet arrived. In fact the only definite statement that Peter was at Avignon is found in the highly unreliable *Gesta Ludovici VIII Francorum regis* of Nicholas of Brai (*Historiens de France*, XVII, 338), but his presence there is strongly suggested in the *Chronicle of Tours* (*ibid.*, XVIII, 316).

[26] *Ibid.* Petit-Dutaillis, *Louis VIII*, pp. 324-325.

[27] The relationship between Henry and Yolande was not very close. By their common descent from Henry I of England they were third cousins twice removed and from William IX of Aquitaine third cousins once removed. Haut-Jussé, *Les papes et les ducs de Bretagne*, I, 113 note 4, 114 note 1.

as compensation. This clause did not envisage the loss of Brittany itself but rather the small fiefs which Peter held of the French crown. Then Henry agreed that if John of Brittany were to die, he would make no claim to the duchy in Yolande's name as long as her father lived. The barons of Brittany were to receive all lands in England to which they had a just claim. The count of La Marche was guaranteed as favorable terms as he had enjoyed before he deserted to Louis. Finally Henry would cross to the continent with an army whenever Peter believed the time to be propitious.[28] In short Henry and Peter concluded a military alliance against the latter's liege lord Louis VIII, but the convention would not go into effect until after Henry's marriage to Yolande. If the pope could be persuaded to grant the necessary dispensation, Peter could look forward to having an English army to assist him in taking vengeance on his enemy King Louis. An alliance of England, Brittany, Champagne, and La Marche might well shake the throne of France.

This formidable coalition had barely taken shape when a totally unexpected event smashed its foundations. On November 8, 1226, King Louis VIII died at Montpensier on his way home from the Midi. He left his realm and his twelve-year-old heir in the care of his wife, Blanche of Castille. Louis' death changed the whole situation as far as Peter was concerned. It seemed certain that the queen regent would be obliged to lean heavily on the support of the young king's relatives and the great barons of France. Among the lords of Capetian blood Peter was outranked only by the late king's half-brother, Count Philip of Boulogne, and his own brother Robert of Dreux. In feudal power he stood second only to his ally Thibaut of Champagne. If she were to rule France successfully, Blanche would need the friendship of the duke of Brittany and would be obliged to buy it at any cost. Peter's wisest course lay in taking measures to enhance his market value as much as possible. Hence what started as a serious plan for rebellion became a grand hoax. The more dangerous Peter made himself, the more Blanche would pay for his friendship.

[28] *Patent rolls, 1225-1232*, pp. 153-154.

The duke of Brittany's attitude was fully shared by the count of La Marche. Hugh of Lusignan's fundamental objects were to make himself absolute master of Poitou and to escape as much as possible from the control of his suzerain. Hence he preferred to give his allegiance to the weakest government he could find. Blanche would need his support enough to pay a good price for it, and she was unlikely to hamper his independence. So Hugh cheerfully joined Peter in building up their joint nuisance value. The two barons ignored the summons to attend the coronation of the new king, Louis IX, and continued their negotiations with England. Peter apparently dispatched a general plan of campaign for the consideration of the English government.[29] But unfortunately for the full success of their schemes the death of Louis VIII had had a far more decisive effect on the attitude of the third member of the baronial league, Thibaut of Champagne. Thibaut had joined the alliance because of his hatred of Louis. While it seems improbable that he had enjoyed Queen Blanche's favors or even seriously hoped to, he certainly had a romantic regard for her.[30] His natural inclination was to rally to the support of the widowed queen and her son. When he received the summons to Louis' coronation, he promptly set out for Reims. Blanche, however, ordered that he should not be admitted to the town.[31] She probably did not credit the current rumor that Thibaut had poisoned her husband, but he had certainly deserted him in the midst of the siege of Avignon. His lady's obduracy forced Count Thibaut to fall back without enthusiasm into the arms of his allies. He remained a nominal member of the rebel league, but his sole object was to obtain Blanche's forgiveness for his conduct toward Louis VIII. His price was a few smiles and kind words.

The situation gave Blanche little freedom of choice as to her course of action. She was far too weak to make a serious attempt to suppress the rebels by force. They would have to be bought—the only question was how high the price would be.

[29] Mousket, II, 562-563. Nangis, *Gesta, Historiens de France*, XX, 312. Wendover, II, 315-316. *Rot. claus.*, II, 206b.

[30] Berger, *Blanche de Castille*, p. 83.

[31] Mousket, II, 564-565.

Her best chance lay in strengthening her own position in order to improve her bargaining power. The queen's first step was to liberate Ferrand of Flanders and thus obtain the permanent friendship of that powerful baron.[32] She then bought the temporary support of her brother-in-law, Philip of Boulogne, by giving him the important Norman castles of Mortain and Lillebonne.[33] Count Robert of Dreux was promised compensation in Normandy if his loyalty to the queen regent cost him his English pension.[34] When she had secured these partisans, Blanche was ready to face the rebellious barons.

On February 20, 1227, the queen mustered her forces at Tours. She carried a potent spiritual buckler in the person of the cardinal of St. Angelo, papal legate to France, but her secular support was not very impressive. The only barons known to have been with her were Philip of Boulogne and Robert of Dreux. The presence of Count Robert indicates the true nature of the expedition. A demonstration of armed force was necessary in order to give Peter and Hugh of Lusignan a decent excuse for deserting their English ally. Meanwhile the allies had gathered at Thouars. Richard of Cornwall and Savary de Mauleon, Henry's seneschal of Poitou, were there with the lords of Brittany and La Marche. Thibaut of Champagne and his associate the count of Bar-le-duc were given safe-conducts by Blanche to enable them to join their allies. They did not enter the town but pitched camp outside the walls. When Blanche and her escort had advanced to Loudon, the stage was set for the negotiations which were to be conducted at a point between the two camps.[35]

There was, of course, no unanimity of purpose among the barons assembled at Thouars. King Henry's lieutenants were anxious to prevent any agreement between the regent and the rebels. Peter and Hugh were ready to be bought, but intended to hold out for a good price. Count Thibaut, however, merely sought the queen's favor. During the course of the negotia-

[32] *Layettes*, II, nos. 1830-1908.
[33] *Ibid.*, no. 1909.
[34] Grant of compensation was made in July 1227. *Ibid.*, V, no. 330.
[35] *Chronicon Sancti Martini Turonensis, Historiens de France*, XVIII, 319-320. Nangis, *Gesta, ibid.*, XX, 312-314.

tions, probably about March 1, the earl of Cornwall and Savary de Mauleon conceived the idea of capturing Thibaut by a surprise attack and thus preventing him from making peace with the regent. Unfortunately Thibaut learned of the plan and escaped to Blanche's camp.[36] Instead of being paid for joining the royal party the count of Champagne was obliged to surrender his rights over the lordships of Breteuil-en-Beauvaisis and Romorantin in exchange for the queen's forgiveness.[37] Thibaut's desertion convinced Peter and Hugh that it was time to make their bargains. The terms of peace were settled through the mediation of Peter's brothers, Robert of Dreux and Henry, archbishop-elect of Reims. It was agreed that Blanche should withdraw her army toward Paris. The duke of Brittany and the count of La Marche would join her on the route to conclude the formal treaty of peace.[38]

On March 16, 1227, Duke Peter met Blanche at Vendôme, and the treaty between them was solemnly sealed. If papal consent could be obtained, Yolande was to be married to King Louis' infant brother, John, count of Anjou and Maine.[39] Peter was to hold Angers, Baugé, and Beaufort until John came of age. If Berengeria, widow of Richard I of England, should die during this period, he would have her town of Le Mans as well. Even if the marriage did not take place or John died before he came of age, Peter would hold these towns for the term agreed upon. When he finally surrendered them, they would be valued by the chancellor of France and the count of Boulogne, and Peter would receive a life pension equivalent to the revenue they had yielded to him. In addition to these lands given him in custody, the duke obtained important fiefs. The fortresses of St. James, Bellême, and La Perrière with their appurtenances which had been placed in his custody by Louis VIII were granted to him outright. If he lost any of these fees through legal proceedings on the part of other claimants, he was guaranteed lands of equal value elsewhere. While it is impossible to make any reliable estimate of the revenues gained

[36] *Ibid.* Morice, *Preuves,* I, 859.

[37] *Layettes,* II, no. 1921.

[38] Mousket, II, 573-574. Morice, *Preuves,* I, 859.

[39] John and Yolande were third cousins as descendants of Louis VI of France.

by Peter under this agreement, it is clear that it made a very respectable provision for his future.[40]   I presume that the intention was to make these grants roughly equal to the English lands which the duke was fairly certain to lose as a result of the treaty.   In return for the concessions made to him Peter accepted some not very onerous obligations.   He swore to serve the king and his mother against " any creature which can live and die."   He would make no agreement of any sort with Henry III, Richard of Cornwall, nor any one at war or truce with King Louis.   Yolande was to be placed in the care of a committee consisting of Philip of Boulogne, Henry, archbishop-elect of Reims, Robert of Dreux, Enguerrand of Coucy, and Mathew of Montmorency.   She was to be in their custody until her future husband reached the age of fourteen and the marriage could be consummated.   If John of Anjou were to die before that time, the barons were bound to return Yolande to Peter.   Finally the duke agreed in advance to a procedure for enforcing the treaty.   If he violated any of its terms, the king should summon him to answer in the royal court.   If he did not obey within forty days, the treaty would no longer be binding on the king, and presumably the lands granted to Peter would be forfeited.[41]

During these early months of 1227 in which Peter had been using his connection with England as a means of extorting concessions from the queen regent, King Henry's advisers had been performing their treaty obligations toward the duke with apparent loyalty.   While the fact that the English government was pressing simultaneous negotiations for the hands of several other ladies casts doubt on the complete sincerity of its promise to marry Henry to Yolande of Brittany, a serious attempt was made to secure a papal dispensation for this match.   Special letters were sent to the bishop of Coventry, who had left England for Rome early in October 1226, ordering him to seek the

---

[40] In 1180 Ranulf of Chester paid a farm of £100 for St. James.   *Magni rotuli scaccarii Normanniae* (ed. Thomas Stapleton, London, 1840), I, 40. Hence its value to Peter must have been well above that sum.   In 1238 the bailliage of Bellême returned £228 for one-third of the year.   *Historiens de France*, XXI, 257.

[41] *Layettes*, II, no. 1922.

pope's consent to the contemplated marriage.[42] As a rule the papacy was duly grateful for the fact that the consanguinity of the royal and noble houses of western Europe placed most of their marriages within the prohibited degrees of relationship. By granting or withholding his dispensation for important marriage alliances the pope could exercise an enormous influence on the politics of Christendom. In this particular case, however, Honorius III found his power most embarrassing. His heart was set on the success of the war against the Albigensian heretics, and he needed the friendship of both the English and French governments. If he consented to the union of Henry and Yolande, he would offend Queen Blanche, while if he refused to sanction the marriage, he would alienate the English regency. Faced with this dilemma, Honorius contrived a delightfully subtle solution. He directed a group of cardinals to write a formal letter to Henry suggesting that the king *facit factum suum* and assuring him that the pope would confirm the result.[43] Although the letter was intentionally vague, it clearly implied that Henry should marry Yolande and present the papacy with the *fait accompli*. Certainly the English government understood the communication in this sense. In the middle of January 1227 an embassy headed by the archbishop of York and the bishop of Carlisle was dispatched to the continent to negotiate with the rebellious French barons and to make a formal demand for Yolande's hand.[44] But they arrived too late. Peter and his friends had already decided to allow Blanche to purchase their support. The duke notified the ambassadors of his agreement with Blanche and returned the letters patent which contained the terms of the treaty of October 1226. The count of La Marche followed Peter's example.[45] The duke of Brittany, however, went even farther than his erstwhile ally.

[42] *Rot. claus.*, II, 138b, 142, 207.

[43] Letter from the bishop of Coventry to Richard, bishop of Chichester. Rymer, *Foedera* (*Record commission*, London, 1816), I, 174.

[44] Wendover, II, 316, 320. *Patent rolls, 1225-1232*, pp. 98-100, 107. *Rot. claus.*, II, 206b.

[45] Wendover, II, 320. The letters embodying Henry's agreements with Peter, Hugh of Lusignan, and Hugh of Thouars were cancelled on the patent roll with the notation *reddite fuerunt*.

He joined the royal captain Humbert of Beaujeu in an expedition against the forces under the command of Earl Richard of Cornwall.[46] On April 6 the English government ordered all Peter's tenants in England to suspend payment of rents. When the return of the archbishop of York made the situation in France absolutely clear, all the duke's lands were seized into the king's hand.[47] For the moment Peter had quit his perch on the international fence and had allied himself definitely with the French crown.

Scourge of the Clerks

Despite his preoccupation during these years with high feudal politics, Peter had not forgotten his enmity for the church. He had been forced to bow before the bishop of Nantes in order to triumph over his barons. Now he was ready for a sweeping assault on the Breton church which he considered to be the last serious obstacle to his complete control over his duchy. The duke made his preparations with considerable skill. Whenever the church became engaged in a major controversy with a feudal potentate, its last resort was an appeal to the royal authority. The pious inclinations of Louis VIII made this a very real threat to Peter's plans. Hence he strove to throw the issue into the national political arena in such a way that Louis would hesitate to support the church against him. In December 1225 Peter held a conference at Thouars with the viscount, the count of La Marche, Amaury of Craon, and a number of minor Poitevin barons. They addressed to Louis VIII a letter complaining of the unbearable exactions of the clergy in their fiefs. Couched in general terms and naming no specific abuses, the letter was a passionate plea for the king's assistance against clerical arrogance. The barons asked Louis to intercede for them with the legate—their pleas to him had obtained merely *verba vacua*.[48] I believe that this letter should be considered as an attempt to justify in advance the policy Peter planned to pursue in Brit-

---

[46] Aubri de Trois-Fontaines, *Chronicon, Monumenta Germaniae historica, Scriptores*, XXIII, 919. Rymer, *Foedera*, I, 186.

[47] *Rot. claus.*, II, 181. Levron, *Catalogue*, no. 108.

[48] *Layettes*, II, no. 1734.

tany. While Louis VIII would be certain to frown on any casual attack on the church, he would be inclined to sympathize with a serious attempt to reduce its secular authority, and he would be extremely unlikely to interfere when the issue was a vital one to the chief barons of the three great districts of Brittany, Poitou, and Anjou. Peter's political instinct was absolutely sound. Louis VIII died before he was called upon to make a decision, but his successor steadfastly refused to aid the church in its controversies with the duke of Brittany.[49]

Peter's plan was to make a triple attack on the Breton church. From at least the time of Pope Gregory VII the clergy had insisted that no layman could lawfully enjoy the tithes intended for the support of the church. Peter claimed that these dues were part of the established property rights of the lay lords. Then in Brittany and several other districts the church maintained that when a man died the local priest had a right to a fixed proportion of his moveable property—one-third if he left neither wife nor child, one-ninth if he did. The duke insisted that this custom was a pure abuse. Finally the principal weapon of the church was the dread power of excommunication, but it could only be truly effective when supported by the secular authorities. If an excommunicate were deprived of his lands and denied all civil rights, he soon came to terms with the church. Peter intended to adopt a regular policy of ignoring excommunications when they were launched against his Breton subjects.[50] In order to put his plan into operation the duke summoned his barons to meet in the monastery of Redon which was noted for its easy customs, its devotion to him, and its resistance to ecclesiastical authority. In this solemn assembly Peter exacted from his willing vassals an oath that they would retain the tithes which they possessed, would prevent the clergy from collecting a part of the goods of the dead, and would grant full rights to excommunicates. Then Peter sent his seneschals to take the oaths of all those who had failed to appear

---

[49] Joinville, *Histoire de Saint Louis* (ed. Natalis de Wailly, *Société de l'histoire de France*, Paris, 1868), pp. 241-242.

[50] For a full discussion of the issues involved see Haut-Jussé, *Les papes et les ducs de Bretagne*, I, 76-79.

at Redon.[51]   Led by its duke, Brittany was in rebellion against the church.

The Breton prelates did not hesitate to accept this challenge. The bishop of Rennes excommunicated the duke and laid an interdict on the ducal demesnes in his diocese.   The bishops of St. Brieuc and Tréguier promptly supported their colleague. Peter's reply was brutal and direct—he ejected the three bishops from their lands and drove them into exile.   When this display of violence moved the bishops of Dol, Vannes, St. Malo, and St. Pol to act against him, the duke drove them too out of Brittany.[52]   The bishop of Quimper, Peter's chancellor and loyal friend, was soon the sole resident member of the episcopate of Brittany.[53]   For the moment the duke was completely triumphant, and the Breton church stood helpless before him. Although papal protests soon rained upon him, it was not until he found himself in new political difficulties in the winter of 1229-1230 that he paid them any heed.

No matter how thoroughly Duke Peter had suppressed all opposition among his clergy and baronage his permanent authority in the duchy was bound to depend on the extent and resources of his demesnes and the number and strength of his castles.   The obedience of the barons had been secured by the sword, and the same means was required to maintain it.   When Peter had succeeded to the duchy, he had found himself fairly well supplied with fortresses in the counties of Vannes and Quimper and notably lacking in this respect elsewhere.   His spoilation of Henry of Avagor had given him control of the chief strongholds of the counties of Tréguier and Lamballe while his occupation of Ploërmel gave him a base in the central hinterland.   His weakness then lay in the counties of Rennes and Nantes.   When one considers that the duke's policy called for continual vacillation between the kings of France and England and hence perpetual danger of war with his Capetian suzerain, the necessity for a firm grip on these two regions becomes evident.   But in 1212 the only ducal fortresses in these counties were the castles and towns of Rennes and Nantes with

[51] Morice, *Preuves*, I, 861-862.
[52] *Ibid.*
[53] Bishop Stephen of Nantes died in February 1227.

the castle of Toufou south of the Loire. For the defense of Brittany from French invasions the duke was forced to rely on the lords of Combourg, Fougères, Vitré, Châteaubriant, and Ancenis. Geoffrey of Châteaubriant was a most devoted adherent, but the other border barons were decidedly lukewarm in their affection for their duke. Hence Peter labored diligently to improve his own strategic resources in the borderland.

In 1214 the duke persuaded John of Dol, lord of Combourg, to entrust his chief castle to him. This was probably intended as a temporary arrangement for the duration of the war between the duke and the houses of Tréguier and Léon, but Peter appears to have kept the fortress until 1234.[54] Combourg was an excellent base for operations against the see of Dol and the baronies of Dinan and Fougères. It would also be an invaluable support to Rennes if Vitré and Fougères failed to halt a French invasion. In 1216 Peter began to build a new stronghold in this same district.[55] This castle, St. Aubin-du-Cormier, was situated in the forest of Rennes midway between that town and Fougères. From St. Aubin it was twenty-seven kilometres to Rennes, twenty to Fougères, thirty-three to Combourg, and twenty-three to Vitré. It could thus threaten the lands of the lords of Fougères and Vitré while forming with Rennes and Combourg a strategic triangle of ducal fortresses. The castle itself consisted of a donjon with two stone-walled enceintes. By flooding a large part of the neighborhood Peter made St. Aubin practically impregnable. To strengthen it still further he founded a new town under its walls and endowed the inhabitants with attractive privileges. In 1225 the barons of Brittany assembled about their duke in Nantes granted the people of St. Aubin freedom from tolls in all their demesne lands.[56] The castle of St. Aubin-du-Cormier was the pride of Peter's heart and was to remain one of the chief strongholds of Brittany throughout the independent existence of the duchy. Finally the duke founded a fortress and town at Le Gâvre some forty

[54] Recueil, no. 88. Nouveau recueil, p. 133.
[55] Levron, Catalogue, no. 29.
[56] Morice, Preuves, I, 853-855.

kilometres northwest of Nantes.[57] The main purpose of this castle was probably to protect and serve as an administrative center for the ducal demesne which included the forest of Gâvre and some outlying territory, but it could be used to control the lords of Blain and Derval. It also gave Peter a base in the region between Nantes and the group of ducal castles lying near Rennes. If the lord of Ancenis proved a traitor, Le Gâvre could cover the western part of the country of Nantes from a French invasion. Thus Peter had a chain of ducal strongholds extending from Toufou to Combourg which could support or if necessary replace the castles of the marcher barons. If the border lords went over to the enemy, their lands could be devastated by the garrisons of these fortresses.

The castles outside Brittany which Peter had obtained from Louis VIII and Queen Blanche fitted neatly into his strategic requirements. The stronghold of St. James served the threefold purpose of acting as an outpost on the northeastern frontier of Brittany, threatening the border barony of Fougères, and giving Peter a convenient base for possible future operations in southwestern Normandy. Bellême was not at the moment of much strategic value to the duke for it was completely isolated from his other castles. Its demesne yielded a good revenue, but it was of little immediate military importance. Bellême might, however, prove extremely useful as a base for future aggression by the ambitious duke. If he continued to hold the chief seat of the counts of Perche, might he not hope to absorb the whole county?[58] The border regions between Maine and Normandy were a promising field for Peter's dreams of territorial power which he might wield when he was no longer duke of Brittany. On the other hand, Champtoceaux and Montfaucon were of immediate strategic importance. The former gave Peter a strong fortress on the Loire through which

[57] *Nouveau recueil*, no. 17. This act of 1296 confirms Peter's grant of privileges to the town. The castle was certainly in existence by 1234. *Testes Domini Andree de Vitriaco contra comitem Britannie*, Archives nationales, Trésor des chartes, J. 646, no. 148.

[58] In 1236 when he married John of Brittany to the daughter of Thibaut of Champagne, Peter obtained for his son the suzerainty of Perche as part of the girl's marriage portion. Jubainville, *Catalogue*, no. 2454.

he could control the commerce of the river and watch the crossings into southeastern Brittany. While at the moment Montfaucon simply gave the duke another fortress which could cooperate with the castle of Toufou in the region south of the Loire, it was to be of immense benefit to him a few years later when he acquired territorial interests in northern Poitou.

Peter was well supplied with proud fortresses which echoed the clanging mail of his garrisons, but the day had passed when a feudal prince of the eminence of the duke of Brittany was content to stow his family in some odd corner of a military stronghold. Their cramped quarters, their permanent garrisons, and their liability to siege and capture in time of war made these strategic castles far from safe and pleasant places for residence. The extent of Peter's fief enabled him to utilize for the protection of his family the most effective known means of defense—distance from danger. For the home of his wife and children and his own official seat he chose a tract of wild moor-land on the peninsula of Rhuis near Vannes. Some five miles along the southern shore from the abbey of St. Gildas where Abelard had found so uncomfortable a refuge from his foes the duke built the castle of Sucinio. A single strong enceinte strengthened by towers still stands, but it has been so extensively rebuilt that it is impossible to reconstruct the castle of Peter's day. A firmly made stone house protected by a moat and palisade would have satisfied the usual requirements of his contemporaries. Peter was using Sucinio as a residence as early as 1218, and shortly after his son John succeeded to the duchy the castle was mentioned as the habitual seat of the dukes of Brittany.[59] It was a perfect place of refuge. Lying deep within the duchy some eighty-seven miles from the French frontier, it stood on a peninsula which could be entered only through the lands of the bishop of Vannes. If by some remote chance an enemy should threaten its walls, the sea lay at hand as a means of escape. Morever Sucinio was in the real Brittany, Gaelic Brittany, whose sons burning with racial patriotism were always the surest auxiliaries of embattled dukes. But this retreat was no dreary refuge. Along the coast stretched moor

[59] *Recueil*, no. 94. Morice, *Preuves*, I, 923-924.

and marsh ideally suited to falconry while the interior of the peninsula was occupied by forests full of game.[60]   Yet despite its attractions Sucinio must have been a wild, desolate spot far removed from the green meadows and yellow grain fields of Peter's native Ile-de-France.

[60] For a description of the site and ruins of Sucinio see Roger Grand, *Mélanges d'archéologie Bretonne* (Paris and Nantes, 1921), pp. 119-141.

III

INTERLUDE OF TREASON

War of Words

The treaty of Vendôme marked the highest pinnacle of power which Peter was destined to reach, but it failed to satisfy his soaring ambition. Two Norman castles, the temporary possession of three Angevin towns, and a life pension were mere bagatelles to one who had dreamed of enjoying the rich county of Flanders. The duke felt that Blanche had bought his allegiance at a bargain price. Furthermore, it seems certain that the principal reason for Peter's willingness to make peace with the queen regent had been his firm conviction that Blanche would be obliged to give him a high place in the government of France. Peter envisaged a realm ruled by the strong if somewhat grasping hands of himself, his brother Robert, and Count Philip of Boulogne. But in the months which followed the conclusion of the treaty the queen showed no inclination to place the king and kingdom at the mercy of young Louis' ambitious and greedy relatives. Sheltered behind the feudal power of the counts of Flanders and Champagne, Blanche governed France by the counsel of the cardinal legate and the old and tried servants of the crown. The joyous prospect of high prestige, rich rewards, and vast power evaporated before Peter's angry eyes.

The duke of Brittany's indignation was fully shared by the counts of Boulogne and Dreux. They had led young Louis to his coronation at Reims and had marched under his banner when he moved against the rebel league. Their only reward had been comparatively insignificant territorial concessions. Instead of seeking their counsel and aid in governing the realm Blanche relied on an Italian prelate, on despised civil servants, and on such recently reformed traitors as Ferrand of Flanders and Thibaut of Champagne. Soon Count Philip and the two Dreux brothers were fiercely discussing their grievances.

Around them rallied a formidable group of friends and relatives—Enguerrand of Coucy, his brothers Robert and Thomas,
Count Henry of Bar-le-duc, and Count Hugh of St. Pol.[1]
Unfortunately while all were agreed that something should be
done, they could not decide on a definite program.   Contemporary rumor credited both Philip of Boulogne and Enguerrand
of Coucy with the ambition to seize the crown of France.[2]   This
seems highly improbable.   Although Count Philip was several
times to be on the brink of open revolt against his royal
nephew, he never actually raised his standard in rebellion.
The lord of Coucy had no conceivable right to the crown.   For
him to hope to step past Philip and the Dreux brothers would
have been utter madness.   It is, however, possible that the
barons considered abducting Louis, declaring themselves his
rightful guardians, and ruling France in his name, but even
this course would probably have been too radical for the con-
scientious count of Boulogne.[3]   There was only one program on
which all the barons could agree with complete enthusiasm—
an attack on Thibaut of Champagne.[4]   He was Queen Blanche's
most powerful friend, yet hostilities against him could not
according to feudal custom be considered as rebellion against
the crown.   Furthermore, he was generally unpopular.   Even
those who did not believe that his desire for the queen had
moved him to poison Louis remembered that he had deserted
his king in the midst of the siege of Avignon.

Peter had his private reasons for encouraging any schemes
against Count Thibaut IV.   The defection of the count of
Champagne from the rebel league had forced him to sell his
friendship to Blanche at too low a price.   It would be pleasant
to take vengeance on Thibaut.   But far more important was
a new idea which was taking shape in Peter's mind.   Thibaut's

[1] Nangis, *Gesta, Historiens de France*, XX, 314. Joinville, p. 26. Jubainville, *Catalogue*, no. 1773. *Récits d'un ménestrel de Reims* (ed. Natalis de
Wailly, *Société de l'histoire de France*, Paris, 1876), p. 176.

[2] *Ibid.*, pp. 176, 179.

[3] The chroniclers suggest that such a plot was behind the fiasco of Montlhéry.
Nangis, *Gesta, Historiens de France*, XX, 314. Joinville, pp. 26-27. Berger,
Blanche de Castille, pp. 110-111.

[4] *Ménestrel de Reims*, pp. 176-177. Mousket, II, 576.

title to the county of Champagne was not impeccable. His father, Thibaut III, had been the second son of Count Henry I. The elder brother, Henry II, had gone to the Holy Land where he married Isabel, queen of Jerusalem, and in her right ruled for five years over the Latin kindom. To Henry and Isabel were born two daughters, Alix and Philippa. But as Queen Isabel had neglected to divorce her first husband, her marriage to Count Henry was of doubtful validity and the legitimacy of their children very questionable. Hence when Henry died in 1197, Thibaut III assumed the dignity of count of Champagne with the full approval of his suzerain Philip Augustus. Unfortunately, however, the only way of definitely establishing the legitimacy or illegitimacy of royal princesses was by a decree of the papal court handed down in the presence of the interested parties. The two sisters had never been formally declared illegitimate and as long as they sedulously avoided Rome, their status would remain in doubt and they could lay claim to the lands of their father. Philippa and her husband had demanded their rights while Thibaut IV was still a minor and had been bought off by Blanche of Navarre, but the elder sister, who was queen dowager of Cyprus, had never advanced her claims. Peter's plan was to marry Alix and join the baronial attack on Thibaut. Even if he failed to obtain Champagne, he could certainly force the count to buy him off at a high price. Perhaps the duke's mind went on to toy with romantic dreams. Only Alix's infant nephew, Conrad of Hohenstaufen, stood between her and the throne of Jerusalem. In the absence of Conrad and his father, the Emperor Frederick II, the custom of the Latin kindom gave the custody of the realm to Alix, and if the boy should die, she would be queen.[5] If all his plans in France went awry, Peter could retire from Brittany to be a great lord d'Outremer. Alix's claims to Champagne and Jerusalem made her the perfect wife for a confirmed adventurer.

Peter's pleasant vision of winning a rich fief in Champagne while breaking the power of Blanche's principal supporter was, however, wrecked by the dilatory ineffectiveness of his baronial

[5] J. L. La Monte, *Feudal monarchy in the Latin kingdom of Jerusalem 1100-1291* (Cambridge, 1932), pp. 70-71, 249.

allies and the queen's influence at Rome. Although as early as July 1227 the plan for an attack on Champagne was so well developed that it had reached Count Thibaut's ears, the barons delayed active operations until the summer of 1229.[6]   Then after invading Thibaut's lands in force, they retired very tamely when Blanche led a royal army to her friend's assistance.[7] Meanwhile as the baronial levies were moving into Champagne, the pope issued letters commanding the patriarch of Jerusalem and the bishop of Le Mans to forbid Peter to marry Alix.[8] Since the duke of Brittany and the queen of Cyprus were second cousins once removed through their common descent from Louis VI of France, the papal prohibition made their union impossible. While Peter continued to encourage the barons to harass Thibaut as a means of weakening Blanche, he no longer had any chance of personal profit from the enterprise. Raids into Champagne might assuage his thirst for vengeance on the queen and Thibaut, but they could not bring him the fiefs he so ardently desired.

Even before the final collapse of his designs on Champagne, Peter had given up hope of attaining his ends by means of the baronial league. He wished either to remove Blanche from the regency or to force her to purchase his friendship at his own price. While the barons might eventually invade Champagne, they clearly lacked the nerve for open revolt against the queen regent. But Peter was far too weak to risk a rebellion unaided. Hence his mind naturally turned to his former ally, Henry III. With an English army at his back and English money in his purse he might well be able to bring Blanche to terms. At a general baronial conference which was held at Corbeil in the early summer of 1229 the duke told his allies of this plan. With the exception of Enguerrand of Coucy who some months later accepted an English pension, the barons declined to take part in negotiations with Henry. They did, however, promise Peter their passive support. If he rose in revolt and they were sum-

    [6] Jubainville, *Catalogue*, no. 1773.   Aubri de Trois-Fontaines, *Monumenta Germaniae historica, Scriptores*, XXIII, 924.

    [7] *Ibid.*   Guillaume de Nangis, *Chronicon* (ed. H. Géraud, *Société de l'histoire de France*, Paris, 1843), I, 177-178.   *Gesta, Historiens de France*, XX, 314.

    [8] Jubainville, *Catalogue*, nos. 1923-1924.

moned to march against him, each baron would join the royal
host with only two knights—the minimum contingent allowed
by custom.[9] They would perform their feudal obligations to the
crown, but Peter had their good will. As the crown's military
resources consisted mainly of the levies brought by the royal
vassals, this agreement limited very decidedly the strength of
the army which Blanche could raise to suppress Peter's revolt.

The duke of Brittany had chosen a highly propitious time to
seek a new alliance with Henry III. The English government
was fully informed about the baronial opposition to Queen
Blanche. Moreover at Christmas 1228 the archbishop of Bordeaux had visited England bearing messages from the barons
of Poitou and Gascony and from many Norman malcontents
who urged Henry to make an expedition to the continent.[10] The
king and his advisers believed that the time had come when a
serious effort to recover the lost continental possessions of the
Plantagenet house might be successful. Hence they were ready
to welcome Peter with unbounded enthusiasm. The duke was
in a position to renew the treaty of October 1226. In May 1227
the newly elevated pope, Gregory IX, had forbidden the marriage of Yolande of Brittany to John of Anjou.[11] Although
Blanche had forced the committee of guardians appointed by
the treaty of Vendôme to swear that despite the papal decision
they would not surrender Yolande to Peter until John of Anjou
reached his fourteenth year, she was technically free to wed.[12]
The queen could prevent Yolande from marrying Henry III
by retaining possession of her person, but she could not keep
Peter from promising her to the English king. If the Anglo-

[9] Joinville, p. 27. Joinville furnishes no date for this meeting. Berger points
out that it must be placed shortly before Peter's revolt, but he believes that the
revolt took place in January 1229. *Blanche de Castille*, pp. 122 and note 3,
125 note 2. For reasons given in appendix I, I have placed the revolt in
January 1230 and have moved the date of the assembly at Corbeil to the summer
of 1229.

[10] Wendover, II, 355-356. *Rot. claus.*, II, 212. *Close rolls, 1227-1231*, p. 232.

[11] *Registres de Grégoire IX* (ed. Lucien Auvray, *Bibliothèque des écoles
françaises d'Athènes et de Rome*, second series), nos. 87-88.

[12] A. Duchesne, *Histoire des maisons de Dreux, de Bar-le-duc, de Luxem-
bourg et de Limbourg, de Plessis, de Richelieu, de Broyes, et de Châteauvillain*
(Paris, 1631), p. 329.

Breton alliance should succeed in breaking Blanche's power, it would be easy to compel her to relinquish Yolande. Sometime during the summer of 1229 Henry and Peter renewed their agreement of October 1226.[13] The English government promised to muster an army and fleet on the channel coast early in the autumn. The duke agreed that he would be on hand to conduct Henry and his troops to the continent—presumably to Brittany.

In October King Henry gathered his army at Portsmouth, and there Peter joined him according to his promise. But Henry's ministers had not collected enough ships to transport the host, and the season was rather far advanced for effective military operations. Peter and the English barons agreed that the expedition should be postponed until after Easter. The duke, however, did homage to Henry for the duchy of Brittany and received his English lands.[14] Peter had at last definitely staked his fortunes on an English alliance. The renewal of the agreement of 1226 had been a violation of the treaty of Vendôme, but the transference to the English king of the homage for Brittany was an act of open rebellion against King Louis. The first could involve no more than the loss of the lands which Peter had acquired at Vendôme, but the penalty for treason could be the confiscation of all the fiefs which the duke held of the French crown. Peter had learned that the pope had forbidden his marriage to Alix of Cyprus. The English alliance was thus the only whole string on his bow. If Henry's aid should enable him to humble Blanche, he might yet satisfy his ambition for power and wealth in France.

While the duke of Brittany had apparently thrown himself wholeheartedly into the alliance with England, he did not abandon his interest in the baronial league. If he could persuade its members to join the Anglo-Breton attack on Blanche, the queen regent was doomed. The fact that Enguerrand of Coucy was for a year the recipient of an English pension shows that he

---

[13] There is no documentary evidence of the renewal of this treaty, but the later relations of Peter and Henry were in accord with its provisions. Certainly they made a treaty at this time, and their actions indicate that it was essentially the same as that of 1226.

[14] Wendover, II, 378-380. *Close rolls, 1227-1231,* pp. 224, 255-256.

at least was capable of contemplating such a course.[15] If, on the other hand, the barons persisted in shrinking from open treason and their support enabled Blanche to triumph over her foes, their friendship could be relied on to mitigate Peter's punishment. Hence the duke continued to encourage his fellow barons to oppose the regent and her government. His arguments have come down to us in the form of poems intended for circulation among the baronial courts. Peter's talented friends attacked on all fronts. One poem is a direct assault on the queen regent. She had used the revenues of the crown for her friends in Spain and Champagne and had kept her son unwed. While scorning the rightful rulers of France, the noble vassals of the crown, she had favored the traitor Thibaut. Even the justice of Rome had been corrupted by her wiles—a reference of course to her friendship with the legate. Another poem was aimed at Count Thibaut. He was a bastard conceived after his father's death and hence unfit to hold his fiefs. Had Louis VIII lived, the traitor count would have been disinherited. He was more competent in medicine than in chivalry—a clear hint at the charge that Thibaut had poisoned Louis VIII. Ruled by Thibaut and his paramour, France was bastardized. Finally a third poem was devoted to an attack on Walter Cornu, archbishop of Sens, who was the chief of the group of royal servants who aided Blanche. The government of France should be conducted by the barons. The king should make peace with his vassals and send the clerks to sing in church. Then the barons of France would soon drive the English from the realm. Louis would do well were he to abandon his confidence in Count Thibaut and return Ferrand of Flanders to his prison cell.[16] Throughout these poems runs one central theme — France should be ruled by its barons. Blanche, Thibaut, and Walter Cornu had scorned the barons' aid and counsel. Blanche was a foreigner who probably slept with Thibaut and possibly with the legate. The count of Champagne was a bastard who had betrayed and poisoned his lord. While there is no way of knowing how effective this propaganda was, it is highly entertaining

[15] *Calendar of liberate rolls, 1226-1240,* p. 161.
[16] *Recueil de chants historiques français depuis le xii* jusqu'au xviii* siècle* (ed. Leroux de Lincy, Paris, 1841), I, 165-178.

and furnishes the historian with the gossip of the baronial courts. But one is amazed at the comparative delicacy of Peter's poetical friends. Another group of Blanche's enemies, the clerks of the University of Paris, were far less squeamish. To them we probably owe the story that in order to confute the current rumor that she was about to bear a child to the legate Blanche was obliged to appear naked before the assembled barons and prelates of France.[17]   Thus the feudal league was based on a mixed foundation of family cohesion, baronial ambition, and musically-slung mud.

By the latter part of November 1229 the French government had learned of the duke of Brittany's negotiations with Henry III.   While Blanche's information about what had happened at Portsmouth in October may not have been very precise, she knew enough to feel certain that Peter had violated the treaty of Vendôme.   The most virulent of her foes had at last given her an opening, and the regent decided to move against him in accordance with the procedure provided by the treaty.   Peter was summoned to appear at Melun on December 30 to explain his behavior.   Either pride or discretion restrained the duke from obeying in person, but he sent representatives.   His words, written a month later, suggest that he would have gone to Melun if the king had planned to be there.   He would deal only with his suzerain—his legates could treat with the king's officers.   At any rate Peter's delegates appeared and protested that the summons was improper as it had not given the duke the requisite forty days notice.   They also presented to the king's representatives a list of injuries which Peter claimed to have suffered at the hands of the regent.[18]   It would be most interesting to know these complaints in detail.   The duke may well have objected to the retention of Yolande after the pope had forbidden her marriage to the queen's son.   Then Peter may have believed that Blanche had been instrumental in persuading the pope to frustrate his plan to wed Alix of Cyprus. But in all probability the list of grievances consisted largely of scurrilous charges similar to those which found expression

---

[17] *Ménestrel de Reims*, pp. 96-99.

[18] This information comes from a letter of Peter's dated January 20, 1230. It will be found in appendix I.

in the poems of Peter's friends. Certainly the document was intended as an instrument of propaganda for the duke's agents demanded that it be shown to the barons. This Blanche refused to do. Taking Peter's refusal to appear in person as contumacy under the treaty, the regent set out to seize the lands which the duke had received at Vendôme. Sometime early in January royal forces occupied Angers, Baugé, and Beaufort in Anjou which apparently offered no serious resistance.

Blanche next turned her eyes toward the great fortress of Bellême. The castle was strong and well garrisoned, but it was isolated from Peter's lands. While two such staunch loyalists as Mathew of Montmorency and Dreux de Mello held respectively Laval and Mayenne, Peter could hardly relieve Bellême if it were attacked by a royal army. The regent, therefore, gathered a force under the immediate command of John Clément, marshal of France, and moved against the castle. Soon after mid-January 1230 Bellême was invested. In the hope of avoiding the expense of siege operations the marshal launched a general assault on the castle walls, but the defenders repulsed it vigorously. Next day he tried mining. Although the miners did not succeed in making a breach, they seriously weakened the outer walls. By the third day the marshal had his siege engines ready. Their fire soon reduced the fortress. When a stone had struck the castellan's residence and killed several people and others had destroyed the keep, the garrison of Bellême capitulated. The mediæval soldier had no affection for desperate, forlorn-hope defenses. The castle of La Perrière had surrendered during the siege of Bellême.[19] While the loss of these two fortresses did little or no harm to Peter's strategic strength, it was a serious blow to his prestige and a feather-in-the-hair of the queen regent.

The seizure of the Angevin lands which he held under the treaty of Vendôme and the attack on Bellême not only con-

---

[19] Nangis, *Chronicon*, I, 179; *Gesta, Historiens de France*, XX, 316. Vincent de Beauvais, *Speculum historiale, ibid.*, XXI, 72. *Querimoniae Normannorum, ibid.*, XXIV, 17-26. For an excellent, if slightly too imaginative, account of the siege of Bellême see E. S. Davison, *Forerunners of Saint Francis and other studies* (Boston, 1927), pp. 287-318. For a discussion of the date of the siege see appendix I.

vinced Peter that it was time to cast aside all pretense of loyalty to the French crown but also gave him the opportunity to do so with some appearance of feudal propriety. His enemies among the barons of France were probably unaware that he had gone so far as to do homage to Henry III for the duchy of Brittany, and his friends could be relied on to forget it. Hence by denying the legality of the summons to Melun he could pose as a vassal gravely injured by his lord. On January 20, 1230, he dispatched a Templar to bear to the king his solemn defiance. The order of the Temple was inclined to favor him, and its members were highly desirable emissaries because of their personal inviolability. In his letter of defiance the duke reviewed his recent relations with the crown. He had been summoned to Melun for December 30, 1229, but the king had refused to meet him in person. Peter had sent representatives who questioned the validity of the summons and presented his list of grievances. Blanche had refused to show his complaints to the barons and had informed his messengers that she would pay no attention to them. The king had then seized the duke's Angevin lands and had laid siege to his castle of Bellême. He had ravaged his lands and slain his men. As the original summons to Melun had been invalid, these attacks were without justification under the procedure laid down by the treaty of Vendôme. The king had injured his vassal. Therefore Peter withdrew from his homage to Louis and formally defied him.[20] Obviously this letter was written neither for the infant king nor for his mother but for the baronage of France. It was Peter's justification of his conduct as a vassal of the crown. Lest Blanche suppress this letter as she had the list of complaints which he had sent to Melun, the duke furnished the Templar who bore the missive to the king with a copy which could be read to the barons. As presumably many of Peter's fellow vassals were with their suzerain in the host investing Bellême, his defense was assured of a good audience. Even if one accepts the duke's account, his argument was rather feeble. He did not claim to be innocent, but merely to have been summoned improperly. Still if he failed and found himself at the king's

---

[20] This letter is printed in appendix I.

mercy, this letter would be a convenient weapon for his friends among the barons. Peter had burned his bridges behind him, but he took care to conceal a shallop or two under the banks of his Rubicon.

Now that he had openly cast his lot with the English king, Peter lost no time in demanding from Henry III compensation for the loss of his fiefs in France. The treaty of 1226 had provided that if the duke lost his French lands because of his service to Henry, he would receive the remainder of the honor of Richmond, and this provision was undoubtedly repeated in the new agreement of October 1229. But in May 1227 while the English government was still enraged by Peter's desertion of its cause, Henry had promised the earl of Chester that he would not be deprived of the castellary of Richmond until he recovered his lands in Normandy.[21] The king was in a difficult position, but he did what he could for Peter. On February 1 the duke received letters patent authorizing his agents in England to levy an aid from his tenants. A few days later Henry returned to Peter the thirty fees of the honor of Richmond below the Humber which had been reserved by the crown in 1219.[22]

The Queen's Foe

King Henry had summoned his host for Easter, but Peter did not await his ally's arrival before starting hostilities. His first move was apparently a raid into southwestern Normandy from his castle of St. James.[23] But more pressing business soon called him to the south of the Loire. Hugh, viscount of Thouars, had just died.[24] His widow Margaret, who was in her own right lady of the baronies of Montaigu and La Garnache,

---

[21] *Patent rolls, 1225-1232,* p. 124.

[22] *Ibid.,* p. 324. *Close rolls, 1227-1231,* p. 297.

[23] *Testes Domini Alani de Assegni contra comitem super dampnis factis in terra uxoris sue,* Archives nationales, Trésor des chartes, J. 646, no. 148. A letter of Peter's dated February 1230 orders his men to protect the abbey of Mont-Saint-Michel during the war. Levron, *Catalogue,* no. 128 and pp. 263-264. This abbey's lands lay in the vicinity of St. James.

[24] His brother Raymond had succeeded him as viscount by May 1230. *Layettes,* II, no. 2055.

claimed the castle of Mareuil-sur-Lay against her brother-in-law
Raymond, the new viscount of Thouars, and the Aunis district
against the count of La Marche.[25]   Margaret was no such prize
as Jeanne of Flanders or Alix of Cyprus, but she had a compact
little fief in northern Poitou adjacent to the southern border of
Brittany.   Peter had chased too many birds in bushes—he resolved to take the one in hand even though its plumage might
not be quite so gay.   Hence he promptly married the lady and
set out to defend her rights.[26]   Peter found northern Poitou in
the state of confusion that was natural to a border district when
war was imminent.   Each baron of the region was trying to
make up his mind which standard to follow.   While the viscount of Thouars and his nephew Guy were inclined to support
the French cause, the latter's brother Aimery, who held by right
of his wife the Breton barony of Machecoul, felt obliged to aid
Peter.   As Aimery's lordship of La Roche-sur-Yon occupied the
country between La Garnache and Mareuil-sur-Lay, his support
made it easy for the duke to seize the disputed fortress.   Soon,
however, the vassals of the count of La Marche moved against
him under the command of Geoffrey of Lusignan, lord of Vouvant.   Peter met them in battle and won an overwhelming victory.   Geoffrey and some thirty of his knights were captured
and consigned to Breton prisons while Peter remained in full
possession of his wife's domains.[27]

On May 3, 1230, Henry III landed at St. Malo.   Peter, who
was still in the south, joined him there three days later.[28]   The
duke and his royal ally then proceeded slowly southward and

---

[25] *Ibid.*, nos. 1963, 2061; III, no. 3628.   *Registres de Grégoire IX,* no. 2673.
For a discussion of Margaret's family and her right to La Garnache and
Montaigu see appendix II.

[26] The date of Peter's marriage to Margaret cannot be established with absolute
certainty.   The first definite reference to her as his wife was in August 1235.
Registres de Grégoire IX, no. 2738. Peter held Mareuil in November 1234.
Layettes, II, no. 2319.   In June 1230 some person unnamed was withholding
Mareuil from Raymond of Thouars. *Ibid.,* no. 2061.   It seems safe to assume
that this was Peter, and that he had already married Margaret.

[27] *Royal and other historical letters illustrative of the reign of Henry III* (ed.
W. W. Shirley, *Rolls series*), no. 309.   *Patent rolls, 1225-1232,* pp. 379, 381,
409-410. *Layettes,* II, nos. 2061, 2062.

[28] Shirley, *Royal letters,* no. 302.

on May 21 arrived at Nantes. On the way they reached an agreement about the castellary of Richmond. Peter held the castle of St. James of which the earls of Chester had once been hereditary constables. He would surrender that stronghold to Ranulf of Chester, and in return the earl would release his claim on Richmond. Henry promptly ordered his justiciar to give Peter's officers possession of Richmond castle and the demesnes and fees of Richmondshire.[29] The duke and king then parted. Henry remained at Nantes where he could watch the Loire valley and negotiate with the barons of Poitou. Peter, accompanied by Ranulf of Chester, went north to Rennes to guard the Breton marches.[30] Rennes was a peculiarly vulnerable point at the moment because of the hostile attitude of André of Vitré.

The house of Vitré was traditionally francophile in its tendencies, and its late chief, André II, had been in high favor with Philip Augustus. He had been given half the ducal demesne of Guérande, and his son had been married to the younger sister of the Duchess Alix.[31] When his father died in 1211, André III was under age, and for some years he was in the custody of his uncle, Alard, lord of Château-Gontier.[32] In 1222 he supported Peter in the war against Amaury of Craon.[33] He even seems to have been prepared to aid his duke against Blanche in 1227.[34] But he and Peter had numerous disagreements. Shortly after André reached his majority, the duke seized his lands in the Guérande—probably on the very reasonable claim that King Philip had had no right to alienate the ducal demesnes. André also was lord of the land in the forest of Rennes where Peter had built his castle of St. Aubin-du-Cormier.[35] Peter had established a market at St. Aubin which gravely injured one on André's domains. Finally André was hereditary vicar of Rennes and as such held some land

---

[29] Wendover, III, 6. *Close rolls, 1227-1231*, p. 410.

[30] Shirley, *Royal letters*, no. 309.

[31] *Cartulaire de Vitré*, nos. 289, 318.

[32] *Testes Domini Andree de Vitriaco*.

[33] *Recueil*, no. 99.

[34] Morice, *Preuves*, I, 859-860.

[35] In 1222 Peter gave André an exchange for this land. *Ibid.*, column 850. Apparently André remained unsatisfied.

there. In improving the fortifications of that town Peter had dug moats and erected works on André's property.[36] Hence when Peter summoned the barons of Brittany to do homage to Henry III, the lord of Vitré refused and declared for King Louis.[37] From Rennes Peter and Earl Ranulf could wage war on André and watch the part of the Breton border which was laid open by his defection.

While Peter raided Normandy, married Margaret of Montaigu, and welcomed Henry III to Brittany, Queen Blanche had been struggling to muster an army for the defense of her son's kingdom. It had been no easy task. Late in December 1229 Thibaut of Champagne and the duke of Lorraine had attacked the lands of the count of Bar, and Ferrand of Flanders had ravaged the county of St. Pol.[38] Even as the English were preparing to cross, the baronial league was gathering its forces for a campaign of vengeance against Thibaut and his friends. Only with the greatest difficulty did Blanche persuade them to make a truce until July 1 so that they could march against the English invader.[39] Perhaps this was the expedition to which Joinville refers when he states that while most of the barons attended their king with only two knights each, Thibaut joined the host with three hundred knights. Certainly Thibaut and his ally Ferrand of Flanders played prominent parts in the campaign.[40] On May 30, 1230, the royal army occupied the Breton stronghold of Clisson on the south side of the Loire.[41] It then proceeded against Peter's castle of Champtoceaux. That fortress and Oudon which lay just across the Loire were soon taken, and Louis laid siege to Ancenis. Meanwhile Henry III

[36] Peter's injuries to André are described in *Testes Domini Andree de Vitriaco.*

[37] Shirley, *Royal letters,* no. 309. Wendover, II, 384.

[38] Aubri de Trois-Fontaines, *Monumenta Germaniae historica, Scriptores,* XXIII, 926. *Chronicon Andrense, ibid.,* XXIV, 769.

[39] Mousket, II, 577. Shirley, *Royal letters,* no. 309.

[40] Jubainville, *Catalogue,* no. 2037. Joinville, p. 27. Joinville's statement has generally been assumed to refer to the expedition against Bellême. Berger, *Blanche de Castille,* p. 24. My reasons for questioning this view will be found in appendix I. The known reluctance of the barons to take part in this campaign convinces me that this was the expedition to which Joinville referred.

[41] *Layettes,* II, no. 2052.

remained peacefully in Nantes and made no attempt to protect his ally's frontier castles.[42]

As her army lay before Ancenis, Blanche decided that the time had come to take definite legal action against Peter as a traitor to his feudal suzerain. While so far she had proceeded against him merely as the violator of the treaty of Vendôme, she would now seek to have the barons of France declare that he had forfeited his fiefs by open treason. As long as an English army lay at Nantes, the duke's condemnation by Louis' court would be of little practical importance, but it would regularize the position of such Breton malcontents as André of Vitré. A baron of Brittany who was unwilling to violate his oath of fealty to the duke, might cheerfully join Louis if Peter were formally deprived of the custody of the duchy. With this end in view thirty prelates and barons of France issued a solemn pronouncement. They had unanimously decided in the presence of King Louis that Peter had by his misdeeds forfeited his right to the custody of Brittany. The vassals of the duchy were therefore released from their oaths of homage and fidelity to him.[43] The impressiveness of this document is greatly deflated, however, when one examines in detail the list of barons who issued it. The prelates consisted of Walter Cornu, archbishop of Sens, and his suffragans of Chartres and Paris. The names of nineteen of the twenty-seven barons are known to us. Thibaut of Champagne and his vassals account for six of these, and Ferrand of Flanders and his men for three more. Five were royal officers headed by the constable, Mathew of Montmorency, and Amaury of Montfort who was soon to succeed him in that office. Another signatory was John, count of Vendôme, who had been forced to ransom himself out of Peter's hands in 1222. But the missing names are more significant than those found on the list. Philip of Boulogne and Hugh of Lusignan are known to have been in the host, yet neither signed this document.[44] Peter's friends were standing

[42] Wendover, II, 384. Nangis, *Chronicon*, I, 180; *Gesta, Historiens de France*, XX, 318. *Layettes*, II, nos. 2056, 2057.

[43] *Layettes*, II, no. 2056.

[44] Mousket, II, 577. Shirley, *Royal letters*, no. 307. *Layettes*, II, no. 2052. The barons whose names are unknown were men of low rank coming at the end of the list.

by him, and Blanche had been forced to be satisfied with his condemnation by a fairly feeble group of prelates and barons. It would serve well enough to ease the consciences of rebelliously inclined Bretons, but it meant nothing as a reflection of the views of the baronage of France.

When she had obtained the decision she sought, Blanche issued in her son's name a proclamation to the barons of Brittany. Peter had been deprived of the custody of the duchy, and they were released from their oaths of fealty. Those who performed their obligations to Louis would be suitably rewarded.[45] Other royal letters announced that André of Vitré had done homage to the king for the fiefs which he had held of Peter. He would remain the king's vassal until John of Brittany reached the age of twenty-one. Meanwhile he would make neither peace nor truce with Peter or Henry III without Louis' consent. During the war his castles would be at the king's disposal to receive his garrisons. In return Louis would give André land worth £500 a year in Normandy. Any losses the lord of Vitré might suffer as a result of his rebellion against Peter would be made good. Louis did, however, specifically refuse to assume responsibility for André's English fiefs or for his land in the Guérande. This would seem to be an admission on the crown's part that Philip's grant had been of doubtful validity. Finally Louis promised that if any of André's castles were besieged by Peter or his allies, he would strive to relieve them as vigorously as if they were royal strongholds. All damage to the castles would be repaired at the king's cost.[46] André had made an excellent bargain, but he sorely needed it. Peter and Ranulf of Chester were at the moment mustering their forces in Rennes for an attack on Vitré, and the whole western portion of André's lands lay at the mercy of the ducal garrisons of Rennes and St. Aubin.[47] Once the royal host withdrew, the lord of Vitré would be in a most unpleasant position.

This withdrawal could not be delayed much longer. The allied barons, friends of Peter and foes of Thibaut, had dared not ignore the summons to the host, but they had obeyed with

[45] *Recueil*, no. 103.
[46] *Layettes*, II, nos. 2057-2059.
[47] Shirley, *Royal letters*, no. 309.

extreme reluctance. The truce with Count Thibaut would expire on July 1. As soon as the barons had performed their forty days service, they would be off to renew their attack on Champagne. Ferrand and Thibaut would have to hasten home to defend their lands, and Blanche could hardly deny them royal assistance.[48] The campaign against Peter and his allies was over for the season. Blanche had captured three or four Breton castles, had won the support of André of Vitré, and had secured Peter's formal condemnation. When one considers that an English army occupied Nantes, and that a good half of the French barons were in avowed sympathy with the rebellious duke, these rather minor successes appear as a great achievement.

Fortunately for Blanche and her son the disloyalty of the French barons was compensated for by the inactivity of the English army. Hubert de Burgh had in years gone by proved himself a brave and determined castellan, but as a general he was cautious to the point of utter incompetence. He made no attempt to advance from Nantes to relieve Peter's beleaguered castles in the Loire valley, and the English army spent the month of June idling in Nantes. In July and August it made a completely futile parade through Poitou and by September 15 was back at Nantes ready to go home. The only effective military operations of the season were conducted by Peter and the earl of Chester, and they were little more than raids in search of booty. Late in September they spent two weeks ravaging Anjou and captured a few castles. In October Earl Ranulf and William II, earl of Pembroke, raided Normandy from St. James and burned the town of Pontorson which belonged to Henry of Avagor.[49] As Henry was at the moment in favor with both Peter and the English king, this was a rather dubious triumph.[50] The presence of the English army had perhaps saved Brittany from a serious French invasion. Beyond that Peter's only profit

---

[48] Wendover, III, 3-4. Mousket, II, 577.

[49] Wendover, III, 8. Wendover states that both these raids took place after Henry left for home, but it seems clear that the later of the two, that on Pontorson, was made while the king was still in Brittany. *Patent rolls, 1225-1232*, p. 408.

[50] *Close rolls, 1227-1231*, p. 443.

from his ally's expedition consisted of £2000 in cash and the assistance of Ranulf of Chester in a series of raids on the French marches.[51]   Late in October King Henry embarked his army and crossed to England.

Before he left Brittany, however, the English king took steps to perpetuate his alliance with Peter.   Pensions from the English exchequer were granted to a number of Breton barons, and others were given the lands which their ancestors had held in England.[52]   Furthermore, the king left in Brittany one hundred knights under the command of William Marshal, earl of Pembroke, and promised to provide the pay for an additional three hundred knights and one hundred serjeants as long as the war lasted.   As soon as he reached England, Henry would give Peter £4,000 toward the cost of these troops.   If a truce was made with the French, he would still support one hundred knights and one hundred serjeants in the duke's service.   Earl Ranulf of Chester remained on the continent to hold his castle of St. James, and Henry promised him a subsidy of £666.   The duke, the marshal, and the earl of Chester were given full authority to do whatever seemed best for the king's interests. Peter was specifically empowered to make a truce with Louis if that seemed the wisest course.[53]   While several years were to pass before the duke succeeded in actually collecting any of the money which Henry had promised him, the two English earls and their men were valuable auxiliaries.

The beginning of the year 1231 saw Peter in a reasonably strong position.   The utter failure of Henry's expedition must have dashed his hopes of removing Blanche from the regency, but he could still hope for eventual peace on favorable terms.   While the queen had succeeded in quelling the war between Thibaut and his enemies, she had not lessened the latter's sympathy for Peter.   The duke had lost some castles in the Loire valley, but he had a firm grip on his new wife's Poitevin fiefs.   If his vassals stood by him, he might well with

[51] *Ibid.*, p. 417.

[52] *Ibid.*, pp. 436, 443.   *Patent rolls, 1225-1232*, pp. 407-408.   *Calendar of liberate rolls, 1226-1240*, p. 210.

[53] *Patent rolls, 1225-1232*, pp. 399, 400, 401, 403.   *Close rolls, 1227-1231*, pp. 450-451.

the assistance of his English allies succeed in defending Brittany against the none too eager royal host. Unfortunately many of the barons of the duchy were unreliable. Peter's victory at Châteaubriant in 1223 had quelled baronial resistance to his will, but it had not convinced his vassals of the correctness of his conception of the ducal prerogative. They were extremely restive and ready to seize any promising opportunity for a new revolt. Peter was fully aware of this situation. In the winter of 1229-1230 he had been alarmed by the possibility that his barons would use the fact that he was excommunicate as an excuse for joining Louis as soon as the war started. The duke had averted this danger by making peace with the church through the intercession of Henry III, but his condemnation by Louis' court in June 1230 gave his vassals an equally good pretext for rebellion.[54] While only André of Vitré had dared to act under the menace of the English army, as soon as Henry withdrew from Brittany other barons sought the royal camp. In January 1231 Oliver of Coëtquen, a minor lord of the Combourg region, did homage to Louis, and in March the king gained the adherence of one of the major barons of the duchy, Ralph of Fougères.[55] Ralph's father had died in 1212 leaving him a minor. When he reached his majority in 1229, Peter exacted an enormous relief before he would receive his homage.[56] As the barons of Brittany questioned the duke's right to demand relief, this alone could account for Ralph's treason. The defection of the lord of Fougères was a serious blow to Peter's strategic position. With the two border baronies of Vitré and Fougères in the king's hands, the royal army had access to the very heart of the county of Rennes. Then in May the new chief of the house of Léon, Guiomar VI, and Henry of Avagor went over to Louis.[57] While these are the only Breton barons whose actual acts of submission have been preserved, a number of others including the lords of Combourg, Châteaugiron, and La Guerche are known to have joined the

---

[54] *Registres de Grégoire IX*, nos. 464, 465. Morice, *Preuves*, I, 909-910.

[55] *Ibid.*, column 873. *Layettes*, II, no. 2128.

[56] *Chronicon Savigniacensi, Historiens de France*, XXIII, 585.

[57] *Layettes*, II, nos. 2135, 2136.

royal party.[58] Of the more important vassals of the duchy only Alan of Rohan, Geoffrey of Châteaubriant, and Richard Marshal, lord of Dinan, remained loyal to their duke.[59] The viscount of Rohan was a peculiarly enthusiastic ally of Peter because he hoped to obtain the lion's share of the viscounty of Porhoët of which his wife and Ralph of Fougères were joint heirs.[60] Queen Blanche was exceedingly generous to the Breton nobles who submitted to the crown. Thus Henry of Avagor received £2,000 of Tours in cash, and he and twenty-five of his knights were taken into the king's pay for the duration of the war. In addition Henry was given a royal castle as a place of safety for his family.[61] These arrangements must have been highly satisfactory to all concerned. The rebel barons were paid for taking vengeance on their duke, and the royal host was strengthened by contingents of hardy Breton knights.

In June 1231 Blanche and her son mustered a formidable army for the invasion of Brittany. In addition to the regular feudal levy the count of Bigorre, the viscount of Limoges, the queen's Breton allies, and many other captains brought paid troops of knights. There was also a strong force of mounted and unmounted serjeants and crossbowmen.[62] After entering Brittany through the friendly baronies of Vitré and Fougères, the army marched toward Peter's stronghold of St. Aubin-du-Cormier. Since they were far too weak to give battle, the duke and the earl of Chester were forced to content themselves with harassing the royal host. Their most successful operation was a flank attack on the king's baggage train which resulted in the capture of nine war horses, two pack horses, three palfreys, and five cart horses. This pleasant little skirmish cost King Louis £147 in compensation to the owners of the horses and

[58] *Paga militum, servientum, et balistariorum equitum et peditum et charrei facta apud Antrain anno domini 1231 mense Julio in crastino Beatae Marie Magadalenae, Historiens de France,* XXI, 220-222.

[59] *Calendar of liberate rolls, 1226-1240,* p. 210.

[60] Morice, *Preuves,* I, 869. Jacques Auberge, *Le cartulaire de la seigneurie de Fougères* (Rennes, 1913), p. 63.

[61] *Layettes,* II, nos. 2135, 2139.

[62] *Paga militum etc., Historiens de France,* XXI, 220-225.

completely satisfied Peter's ardor for battle.[63] When the royal army reached the walls of St. Aubin, the duke and his English colleague asked for a three-year truce. With the fate of Bellême fresh in his mind Peter had no desire to see his favorite fortress undergo the rigors of a siege. Despite Blanche's anxiety to punish the rebellious duke of Brittany she was probably glad to accept his offer of a truce. St. Aubin-du-Cormier was a magnificent fortress, and in it were two of the most noted captains of the day, Peter and Ranulf of Chester. To reduce this castle would be a slow and costly process, and even when it had been accomplished Rennes and Combourg would still threaten the region. The wisest course for the regent was to stop the war while she had the advantage. But whatever the queen's wishes may have been, she can have had little real choice in the matter. The number and importance of Peter's friends and relatives made it out of the question to press the campaign against him once he had sued for peace. Hence on July 4 a truce for three years was solemnly concluded, and three weeks later the royal army was disbanded.[64] The fact that Philip of Boulogne and Henry of Dreux, archbishop of Reims, were the ambassadors who actually negotiated the truce in King Louis' name shows how helpless Blanche was before Peter's baronial friends.[65]

As the two French negotiators were partisans of Peter, it seems safe to conclude that the terms of the truce represented the minimum requirements of Blanche. The queen apparently insisted that in so far as it was possible Peter should be prevented from conspiring with his baronial friends and from taking vengeance on the king's allies in Brittany. Since the first of these objects involved simply the personal conduct of Peter of Dreux while the second concerned the official policy of the duke of Brittany, two distinct agreements were negotiated. In the compact dealing with his behavior as a private individual Peter promised that as long as the truce lasted he

[63] *Ibid.*, pp. 222-223. Wendover, III, 13.

[64] *Paga militum etc., Historiens de France*, XXI, 220. *Layettes*, II, no. 2141. This is the truce between Louis and Henry III. I assume that Peter made his private truce on the same day.

[65] Wendover, III, 13.

would not cross a line drawn from Mortain in Normandy through Domfront, Vendôme, Saumur, Loudon, and Poitiers. He also agreed to stay out of the lands of Hugh of Lusignan and to enter no royal castle or town.[66]   Thus the duke was confined to Brittany and the districts adjacent to its frontiers. While the fact that Peter had done liege homage to Henry III made it perfectly reasonable that he should be banned from French territory, this treaty could not hamper his activities very much.   He could send messages to his baronial associates or meet them in a region near the Breton border.   As Mortain belonged to Philip of Boulogne, such a conference could easily be arranged.   Blanche must have realized how flimsy were the bonds with which she was binding her enemy, but at the moment any restriction on Peter's activities seemed worthwhile. The queen believed, probably rightly, that the duke of Brittany was responsible for the baronial opposition to her government, the scurrilous attacks on the characters of herself and her associates, and the invasions of the lands of her ally Count Thibaut. He had certainly arranged the expedition of Henry III.   In short Blanche felt that Peter was the source of all her woes. To keep him out of France would assuage her injured feelings even if it brought no more practical result.   Unfortunately the second agreement, the one which dealt with Peter's conduct as duke of Brittany, has been lost, but Le Baud claims to have seen it and a reasonably satisfactory reconstruction of it can be made from his account supported by other evidence.[67]   The duke promised that as long as the truce endured he would make no attempt to punish the Breton barons who had supported King Louis.   Furthermore he was to return to his rebellious vassals all lands of which he had despoiled them during the course of the war.   The duke could, however, retain the castles

---

[66] *Layettes*, II, no. 2144.

[67] Pierre le Baud, *Histoire de Bretagne avec les chroniques des maisons de Vitré et de Laval* (ed. le Sieur d'Hozier, Paris, 1638), p. 233. A large amount of varied information about the terms of this truce can be culled from the investigations into their observance which Louis conducted in 1235. *Nouveau recueil*, nos. 3-7. Archives nationales, Trésor des chartes, J. 626, no. 148. For a discussion of these documents see Sidney Painter, "Documents on the history of Brittany in the time of St. Louis," *Speculum*, XI (1936), 470-472.

which he had captured. St. Aubin-du-Cormier and possibly Champtoceaux were to be surrendered to Count Philip of Boulogne.[68] If Peter violated the terms of the truce, these castles were to be turned over to the king. Finally Louis was to choose seven barons of Brittany who were to swear that if the duke did not keep his promises, they would aid the king against him. While the primary purpose of this treaty was to protect Louis' Breton allies, Blanche may have hoped that Peter would violate it and she would gain possession of St. Aubin. The whole arrangement, however, had one serious weakness from the queen's point of view—its enforcement rested in the hands of the count of Boulogne. Blanche had mustered an army mighty enough to overawe Peter and Ranulf of Chester, but she could not cope with the duke of Brittany's partisans among the magnates of France.

Humbled Rebel

Despite the favorable terms of the truce, Peter must have realized in the summer of 1231 that his major ambitions had been completely frustrated. By his marriage to Margaret of Montaigu he had renounced all hope of securing one of the great fiefs of France. There was no longer any chance of removing Blanche from power. His baronial allies would join him in a private war or use their influence in his favor at court, but they insisted on scrupulous observance of their obligations to Louis. English aid had proved a complete illusion. Unless some miracle intervened, Peter would have to make peace on Blanche's terms when the truce expired. Hence his policy for the next three years was largely defensive. His aim was to build up his bargaining power as much as possible. By maintaining his alliance with England he could draw useful subsidies from Henry's exchequer, enjoy the rich revenues of the honor of Richmond, and hold the possibility of a new invasion as a permanent threat over the French government. Meanwhile he could seek to extend his circle of friends and allies

---

[68] A papal letter mentions Champtoceaux as a castle pledged by Peter. *Registres de Grégoire IX*, no. 1710.

among the French barons and attempt to regain the mastery of his duchy.

Even before the royal army had been disbanded after the conclusion of the truce of St. Aubin, an opportunity appeared which might allow Peter to increase enormously his influence over the baronage of France. On July 11, 1231, the death of Agnes, countess of Champagne, left Count Thibaut a widower.[69] Soon Peter's friends suggested that the enmity between the houses of Dreux and Champagne could be ended by a marriage between Thibaut and Yolande of Brittany. The idea appealed to Thibaut. He was extremely tired of living in perpetual dread of an invasion of his lands by most of his neighbors, and the marriage to Yolande would win him the friendship of Burgundy, Dreux, Coucy, St. Pol, and Bar-le-duc.[70] Then it is likely that the thirty-year-old count who was an experienced connoisseur of female charm had already been attracted by the fresh young girl who had just reached the marriageable age of twelve or thirteen.[71] Both politically and romantically it was an ideal match from Thibaut's point of view. Unfortunately there were two serious obstacles to its consummation. Peter had promised his daughter to Henry III, and Blanche would be certain to oppose an alliance between Brittany and Champagne. But Peter had gone to England as soon as he had made the truce of St. Aubin.[72] While he may have known of the plan to marry Yolande to Thibaut, no one could accuse him of being an active party to it. The duke did not even have possession of his daughter's person for she was still in the custody of the guardians named in the treaty of Vendôme.[73] There seems little doubt that it was two of these guardians, the count of Dreux and the archbishop of Reims, who initiated the scheme to marry Yolande to Thibaut. Although the guardians had sworn not to surrender her to Peter, they had not promised not to find her a husband. Then Blanche's loyal friend, Mathew

---

[69] Aubri de Trois-Fontaines, *Monumenta Germaniae historica, Scriptores,* XXIII, 929.

[70] See genealogical chart no. 1.

[71] *Chansons de Thibaut de Champagne,* no. 50.

[72] Wendover, III, 13.

[73] Duchesne, *Maison de Dreux,* p. 329. *Registres de Grégoire IX,* no. 1710.

of Montmorency, had recently died, and Philip of Boulogne was not a man to hamper the plans of the house of Dreux. In short Yolande's two uncles were ready to marry her to Thibaut without the consent of either the king or the girl's father. They agreed to conduct her to the abbey of Val-Secret. Thibaut would wait nearby in his fortress of Château-Thierry until they summoned him to the wedding.[74]

The count of Champagne was apparently somewhat troubled by the possible adverse effect of this highly questionable procedure on baronial opinion. As he was one of the most noted trouvères of his day, he decided to write a poem in justification of his contemplated marriage. It was composed in the form of a dialogue between Thibaut himself and a companion named Robert. Thibaut complains to Robert that *Perron,* who has the heart of a traitor and the face of a thief, plans to marry his charming daughter to a *si loigtaing baron.* Robert replies that Thibaut will be to blame if the girl weds her far-away suitor. He loves her himself and has the power to prevent the marriage. Thibaut then assures Robert that he would rather lose all his lands than allow her to leave for a distant country. He only wishes that he might lie by her side for one night. Robert hopes that God may grant Thibaut his heart's desire.[75] In short Thibaut will marry Yolande to save her from exile to England as the wife of Henry III. His companion, who is probably Yolande's uncle Count Robert of Dreux, encourages him. When this poem was recited in the castle-halls of France, no baron of sentiment could fail to sympathize with the two genial conspirators. Unfortunately, however, Queen Blanche either never heard the poem or was proof against its appeal. As count Thibaut rode out of Château-Thierry on his way to Val-Secret, he was met by a royal messenger who bore King Louis' letters forbidding his marriage to Yolande.[76] Some months later a papal prohibition supported the king's command.[77] Thibaut bowed to his suzerain's will and married the

---

[74] Joinville, p. 29.

[75] *Chansons de Thibaut de Champagne,* no. 50. See S. Painter, "The historical setting of *Robert veez de Perron," Modern language notes,* LII (1937), 83-87.

[76] Joinville, p. 29.

[77] *Registres de Grégoire IX,* no. 789.

daughter of the lord of Bourbon who was a staunch friend of the crown. Blanche had accomplished her end—for the time being at least she had prevented an alliance between Thibaut and the house of Dreux.

While his brothers were attempting to marry his daughter to Thibaut of Champagne, Peter himself was attending to his interests across the channel. Soon after the conclusion of the truce of St. Aubin, he set out for England in the company of Earl Ranulf of Chester and Richard Marshal, lord of the Breton barony of Dinan.[78] The death of his brother William in the spring of 1231 had made Richard heir to all the vast possessions of the Marshal family in England, Wales, and Ireland, but he was viewed with suspicion by Henry's advisers. He had been educated at the French court and at his mother's death had done homage to Philip Augustus for the family lordships of Longueville and Orbec in Normandy. A few years later he had married Gervase, lady of Dinan.[79] Henry's counselors were most unwilling to believe that the lord of Longueville and Dinan would become a loyal vassal of the English crown. Late in July or early in August Peter and his companions found King Henry at Maud's Castle in the Welsh marches, and on August 8 Henry invested Richard with his late brother's fiefs.[80] It seems likely that Peter's influence had much to do with the king's decision to recognize Richard as earl of Pembroke. Certainly it was to the duke's interest to have a loyal friend and vassal among the great barons of England. In fact within two months he was in need of such support. A plan was afoot to marry the young king to a sister of King Alexander of Scotland. While Peter may have known of his brothers' efforts to wed Yolande to Thibaut of Champagne, he was unwilling to surrender his status as Henry's prospective father-in-law until his daughter was actually married to someone else. He therefore joined forces with the members of the English baronage who

---

[78] Wendover, III, 13.

[79] Painter, *William Marshal*, pp. 279-280. *Layettes*, I, no. 1397. Morice, *Preuves*, I, 851.

[80] Wendover, III, 13-14. *Close rolls, 1227-1231*, p. 541. Wendover's story of Richard's trip to Ireland is clearly impossible. He did not leave France until after July 4 and received his lands on August 8.

opposed the match. Peter and his friends were successful, and Henry remained for three more years the very nominal fiancé of Yolande of Brittany.[81] The duke then turned his attention to collecting the subsidy which King Henry had promised him, but the depleted state of the English exchequer made that a most difficult task. Roger of Wendover states that he sailed home with £3,333 in cash. Unfortunately he makes exactly the same statement with regard to Peter's visit to English in the autumn of 1229, and neither payment can be found on the rolls.[82] I suspect that the duke's purse bulged with nothing more than rosy promises.

Duke Peter made two or three more visits to England during the truce. He was clearly in high favor at the English court. King Henry welcomed him with extreme enthusiasm and insisted on defraying all his expenses while he was in England. He even forbade his subjects to sell the duke or his entourage supplies of any sort.[83] But much as Peter undoubtedly appreciated free meals, he was looking for cash in large sums, and this Henry found hard to provide. On March 10, 1232, the king promised to pay him £2,000 two weeks after Easter. The Temple and the Hospital guaranteed this payment in return for sufficient security deposited in their coffers. Apparently Peter received this money in June or July.[84] On September 25 of the same year the king announced that he would pay £4,000 at Michaelmas.[85] As none of this actually appeared, Peter crossed to England in April 1233. On April 25 a general financial convention was made. Henry promised the duke £6,666 to cover all the arrears of the promised subsidies, and £4,000 of this was paid at once. Furthermore, Peter received £1,200 to reimburse him for the money he had spent in maintaining the castle of St. James which had come into his care when Earl Ranulf of Chester died in October 1232. Then four Breton barons received the arrears of their English pensions, and several more were paid compensation for lands in Anjou which

[81] Wendover, III, 15. *Close rolls, 1231-1234*, p. 151.
[82] Wendover, II, 380; III, 15.
[83] *Close rolls, 1231-1234*, p. 128.
[84] *Patent rolls, 1225-1232*, pp. 465-466, 490.
[85] *Ibid.*, p. 501.

they had lost through their service to Henry.[86]   In short Peter had collected for himself £5,200 in cash and smaller amounts for his vassals.   The duke, however, believed in making the most of his opportunities as he foresaw that the silver harvest would soon end.   In the spring of 1234 he pointed out to Henry that the truce was almost over and he was in need of money to carry on the war.   Henry promised him £4,382.   He also agreed to send 60 English knights to garrison St. James from June 24 to September 14.   Finally the king promised to give Peter additional compensation in England for the French fiefs which he had lost.[87]   This was the last convention between Henry and Peter.   The knights duly arrived on the continent, but only £2,000 of the money was paid.[88]   Still Peter had not done so badly.   During the years 1230-1234 he certainly actually received £10,000 in straight subsidies.   If the two gifts recorded by Roger of Wendover were really made the total must have reached £16,666.   In addition the duke was receiving about £1,200 a year from the honor of Richmond and some revenue from the lands which Henry had given him as compensation for his losses in France.[89]   Thus Peter's average annual income from England during this five-year period was certainly about £3,333 and may have reached £4,666.

Throughout the major part of the three-year truce Peter's conduct in Brittany was almost exemplary.   While it is true that the duke retained improperly the lands of a sister of André of Vitré and the Guérande and other outlying possessions of André himself, in general he respected the terms of the agreement made at St. Aubin.[90]   But one must not conclude that Peter had suddenly grown virtuous.   He was simply disinclined to embarrass his friend Count Philip of Boulogne who had been charged by King Louis with the task of supervising the

---

[86] *Calendar of liberate rolls, 1226-1240*, pp. 208, 210, 239.

[87] *Close rolls, 1231-1234*, p. 556.

[88] *Ibid.*, pp. 443, 464, 558, 559, 564.

[89] Pipe roll 12 Henry III, cited in Jacques Levron, "Pierre Mauclerc, duc de Bretagne," *Mémoires de la société d'histoire et d'archéologie de Bretagne*, XIV (1933), XV (1934), p. 97.   The pages are numbered consecutively through the two sections of this work.   This figure agrees with an estimate made in 1261.   *Calendar of patent rolls, 1258-1266*, p. 160.

[90] Archives nationales, Trésor des chartes, J. 626, no. 148.

execution of the treaty. Although Philip's attitude cannot be described as austere since he cheerfully accepted £400 from Henry III through Peter, he seems to have made an honest effort to enforce the terms of the truce.[91] But the whole situation was changed when Count Philip died suddenly in the winter of 1233-1234. The duke regained his castle of St. Aubin and set to work to revenge himself on his rebellious vassals. The lands of Guiomar of Léon, Henry of Avagor, John of Dol, André of Vitré, and many lesser men were thoroughly ravaged. For good measure the see of Dol and several abbeys were plundered by the duke's men.[92] Peter's enemies found no respite until the expiration of the truce temporarily diverted his attention to his more dangerous opponent, Louis of France.

The truce of St. Aubin was due to expire on June 24, 1234, and both sides made extensive preparations for the hostilities which were certain to ensue. Peter received considerable reinforcements from England. King Henry sent to Brittany 90 English knights and 2,000 Welsh mercenaries and commanded his seneschal of Gascony to assist Peter in the defense of the duchy.[93] The duke, however, was fully aware that the game was finished. Nothing short of an English expeditionary force as large as the one which had crossed to Brittany in 1230 could enable him to hold his own against the mighty host which King Louis was mustering against him. Two weeks before the end of the truce it was common knowledge in France that Peter was ready to come to terms with the king.[94] But feudal propriety demanded that the duke of Brittany should find a reasonable excuse before deserting the allegiance of Henry III. Hence Louis was forced to make a military demonstration which could serve as the pretext for Peter's submission. As soon as the truce came to an end, three royal armies moved against Brittany. In the north St. James was invested, in the center Châteaubriant was besieged and captured, while in the

---

[91] *Ibid. Calendar of liberate rolls, 1226-1240*, p. 210.

[92] Inquests of 1235. *Nouveau recueil*, nos. 3-7. Archives nationales, Trésor des chartes, J. 626, no. 148.

[93] *Close rolls, 1231-1234*, pp. 556, 558, 559. *Ibid., 1234-1237*, pp. 169-170. Wendover, III, 93. *Nouveau recueil*, pp. 127, 130.

[94] *Layettes*, II, no. 2285.

Loire valley Oudon and Champtoceaux capitulated to the king's troops.[95] The campaign lasted about a month. Sometime during August Peter met Louis at Oudon and obtained a truce until November 15. This agreement provided that the duke should go to England to seek the aid of Henry III. If the English king did not cross to Brittany in person before the end of the truce, Peter would surrender to Louis. This procedure was in accord with contemporary custom. Peter had done homage to Henry III for Brittany. When a vassal was hard pressed by his foes, he was expected to ask his lord to protect him. If the latter failed to do so, the vassal was free to shift his allegiance. Peter also promised King Louis that he would not injure his Breton vassals during the truce. As a guarantee that he would fulfill his agreements, the duke surrendered three castles, St. Aubin, Champtoceaux, and Mareuil-sur-Lay. His younger brother, Count John of Macon, pledged all his lands that Peter would keep the truce, and the duke of Burgundy and two other barons became his pledges for fixed sums.[96] The days had passed when Peter could rely on his baronial friends to secure for him easy terms. Philip of Boulogne and Robert of Dreux had both died during the previous winter, and their loss seriously weakened the ranks of the duke's partisans. Moreover Louis had reached his twenty-first year, and while Blanche in all probability still governed his policy, the enormous prestige of a king of full age was a strong deterrent to baronial opposition to the government.

Although the terms of this truce of August 1234 were far more effective from the point of view of the royal government than those arranged at St. Aubin in July 1231, they gave less real protection to the Bretons who had supported King Louis. During the years after the conclusion of the earlier treaty the actual presence in the duchy of Philip of Boulogne who was responsible for enforcing the truce had served to guard the

[95] Wendover, III, 93. *Annales Sancti Florentii Salmurensis* in *Recueil d'annales Angevines et Vendomoises* (ed. Louis Halphen, Paris, 1903), p. 125. Mousket, II, 589. *Querimoniae, Historiens de France*, XXIV, 31, 58, 82, 104. Some of these complaints made in 1247 may refer to the compaigns of 1230-1231. Berger, *Blanche de Castille,* p. 236 and note 8.

[96] Wendover, III, 94. *Layettes,* II, nos. 2302-2306.

rebellious barons of Brittany from their duke's anger.[97]   But the treaty of August 1234 did not provide for a resident supervisor.   Once Louis had withdrawn his army from Brittany, he had no official source of information on the affairs of the duchy. Moreover any formal procedure against Peter or his pledges for violation of the terms of the truce would take time.   The king might be able to punish the duke if he mistreated his vassals, but he could not prevent him from doing so.   Peter on his side was perfectly willing to gamble on his ability to avoid the eventual consequences of violating the truce if it enabled him to take immediate vengeance on his enemies and enjoy the profits of plundering their lands.   Hence no sooner had the truce been made than he sent his troops to resume the ravaging of the estates belonging to his disloyal vassals.   The duke even turned loose his fierce Welsh mercenaries on the see of Dol and adjacent districts.[98]   Only after he had thoroughly devastated the fiefs of Louis' Breton partisans did Peter send home his English troops and prepare to proceed in person to King Henry's court.

When Peter arrived in England, he formally asked King Henry to protect Brittany as a fief held of the English crown. The king declined to cross the sea himself, but he offered to send four earls with enough troops to defend the duchy.   According to feudal custom this was a satisfactory answer.   Peter, however, had promised to surrender to Louis unless Henry came to his aid in person.   As a matter of fact both Louis and Peter had realized that the English king would not cross to Brittany before November 15, and they were simply seeking to furnish the duke with a decent excuse for renouncing his allegiance to Henry.   But the fact that he had committed himself to making submission to the French king did not deter Peter from trying to get some more money from the English treasury.   He told Henry that he had used all his spare funds to buy the truce.   He had spent £10,000 fighting King Henry's war—it would be only fair to reimburse him.   The king turned deaf ears to this plea.   He had expended large sums on Peter

---

[97] *Nouveau recueil,* p. 123.

[98] *Ibid.,* nos. 3-7. Archives nationales, Trésor des chartes, J. 626, no. 148.

with no appreciable result. If the duke remained loyal, he would send the four earls and the troops, but the subsidies were definitely at an end.[99]

Roger of Wendover clearly implies that Henry suspected that Peter had misapplied the funds which had been given to him for carrying on the war against Louis. This suggestion leads to a question which is of very decided interest to Peter's biographer. Did the duke make a financial profit out of his otherwise fruitless struggle with the French crown or did he, as M. Levron believes, drain to the dregs his own resources and those of his duchy in order to maintain the essentially hopeless contest?[100] While lack of information as to the extent and cost of Peter's military activities makes it impossible to answer this question categorically, it seems worthwhile to attempt to reach some conclusion. Wendover's opinion must be given great weight. He disliked and distrusted Peter, but he also knew in a general way how much fighting the duke had done and its probable cost. The scanty evidence available tends to support Wendover's view. During the period in which he was Henry's ally Peter received direct subsidies amounting to between £10,000 and £16,000 sterling in addition to £4,800 sterling drawn from the honor of Richmond. Then Henry supplied about £1,000 a year for the maintenance of the castle of St. James and furnished 90 knights and 2,000 Welsh for the campaign of 1234. Although the alliance between England and Brittany was in force from October 1229 to November 1234, there were only about nineteen months of actual hostilities. The duke of Brittany did not engage in any large scale military operations. The tactics employed by Peter and the earl of Chester in 1231 and by Peter alone in 1234 indicate that they had very small forces at their disposal. In short the duke's military expenditures cannot have been very large. Yet the money which he received from England would have been enough to pay for three expeditions as costly as the one which

---

[99] Wendover, III, 94.

[100] " Le règne de Mauclerc avait ruiné la Bretagne." Levron, *Catalogue*, p. 191. For a discussion of M. Levron's account of the financial relations between Peter and Henry III see appendix IV.

Louis led against Brittany in 1231.[101] Hence it seems highly
improbable that Peter's contest with Louis cost more than he
received from England, and he may have made an actual profit
from the alliance. Then the duke repeatedly plundered the
lands of his enemies in Brittany and enjoyed the estates of
several of them for considerable periods. On the whole it
seems distinctly likely that Peter succeeded in turning his
politically futile struggle with the French crown into a financial
bonzana.

In November 1234 as the brief truce drew toward its end,
Peter journeyed to Paris to make his peace with Blanche and
her son. The terms which were imposed on the defeated duke
were embodied in two separate agreements one of which dealt
with Peter's relations with his vassals while the other concerned
his obligations toward the crown. Blanche had learned how
severely the Breton partisans of King Louis had suffered during
the recent truce, and she was determined to force the duke to
make them adequate reparation. Peter was obliged to swear
that in all the questions at issue between himself and his rebellious vassals he would accept and carry out the commands of
the royal government. As a guarantee that he would keep this
promise he surrendered the castles of Champtoceaux, Mareuil-
sur-Lay, and St. Aubin-du-Cormier. If Peter fulfilled the terms
of the treaty, these fortresses would be returned to him at
Easter 1238.[102] Thus the duke bound himself without any
qualification to accept the decision of the queen and her son
in regard to the claims made against him by his Breton enemies.
In the second agreement Peter swore fidelity to Louis and
Blanche " against any creature that can live and die." He also
promised not to make any treaty with Henry III, Richard of
Cornwall, or any one at war or truce with the French crown.
Then the duke formally renounced all claim to St. James,
Bellême, La Perrière, and the lands in Maine and Anjou which
he had been granted by the treaty of Vendôme. By Christmas
time he would return the charters by which Louis had given

---

[101] The campaign of 1231 apparently cost Louis about £18,000 of Paris.
Historiens de France, XXI, 226. £18,000 of Paris was roughly equivalent to
£6,000 sterling.

[102] *Layettes*, II, no. 2319.

him those fiefs.[103]   Peter was once more a vassal of the French crown—a sadly humiliated vassal.

Peter had lost the game—the house of Capet had proved too strong for that of Dreux.   He had been recklessly over-optimistic.   His hope that the barons of France could be combined against the regent and that Henry III would furnish effective aid had proved pure illusions.   But fate also had been unkind. The deaths in 1234 of Philip of Boulogne and Robert of Dreux had deprived him of his most influential friends at court.   Had they still lived, he might well have obtained better terms.   As it was he lost all he had gained by the treaty of Vendôme, and Henry III was certain to confiscate his English lands.   Worse yet the terms of the treaty permitted Blanche to make him impotent in his own duchy.   Fortunately his reign as duke of Brittany had only three years to run, and nothing Blanche might force him to do could bind his son.   When one is tempted to criticize Peter as a reckless gambler who staked all he possessed on wild, ambitious schemes, one must remember that he did not own and could not lose his main stake, Brittany.   Duke John would come into his duchy with every right and possession which his mother had had at her death.   Peter had gambled at his own risk not that of his heirs.

Moreover while he had failed to gain the high stakes for which he played, Peter had succeeded in making moderately satisfactory provision for his own future.   It seems likely that his financial transactions with Henry III and his industrious plundering of his Breton enemies had yielded him a good store of ready money.   Then his marriage to Margaret of Montaigu had secured him a territorial position of some importance. The lord of La Garnache and Montaigu would not be a great baron of France, but he would be a dominant power in northern Poitou.   If during the three years in which he would still be duke of Brittany he could effectively use the resources of the duchy to improve his position south of the Loire, Peter could retire with a very pleasant endowment in lands, castles, and revenues.

---

[103] *Ibid.*, no. 2320.

IV

A RETIRING DUKE

By Aid of St. Peter

The spring of 1235 saw the ladder by which Peter had hoped to climb to the goal set by his ambition lying in fragments about him. His submission to the French crown had cost him his alliance with England. The subsidies from King Henry's treasury had ceased, and the revenues of the honor of Richmond flowed into other pockets than his.[1] No longer could he threaten the frontiers of France and his own rebellious vassals with English knights and fierce Welsh mercenaries. Then the deaths of Philip of Boulogne and Robert of Dreux had deprived him of his two most potent supporters in France. While he still had close friends and ready allies in the French baronage, they were not in a position to exert much influence on Blanche and her son. Even more discouraging was the situation which faced him in his own duchy. The peace between Peter and the church which Henry III had arranged in 1230 had not proved very durable, and by 1235 the duke was again in conflict with most of the Breton bishops. Then not only did King Louis feel obligated to see that reparation was made to his partisans in Brittany for the injuries which Peter had inflicted on them, but the duke had solemnly promised to accept and carry out the king's decisions in this respect. Finally Peter of Dreux was in as uncomfortable a position as Peter, duke of Brittany. His submission to Louis and Blanche had gravely injured his personal prestige. He had lost a fair part of his private domains, and two of the most important castles which were left to him were held by the king as pledges for his good conduct. Parts of his wife's possessions were claimed by the count of La Marche and the viscount of Thouars. In less than three years John of Brittany would be of age. If

---

[1] Wendover, III, 94-95. *Close rolls, 1234-1237*, pp. 129, 146, 310-311.

89

Peter was to recoup his own fortunes and those of his house, he would have to work rapidly, diligently, and skillfully.

The duke's greatest need was a powerful ally to serve as a bulwark against the French crown and the prelates and barons of his duchy. The search for this ally required no great perspicacity—the only two possibilities were Westminster and Rome. As the former had already failed him, Peter turned toward the head of Christendom. Early in the autumn of 1234 before the conclusion of his final treaty with Louis the duke informed the pope that he was willing to appear in person before the papal curia to answer the complaints of the bishops of Brittany.[2] Peter could hardly have chosen a more auspicious moment to court Gregory's favor. Ever since the flaming words of Urban II had first moved the chivalry of Europe to hurl itself against the infidel masters of Palestine, each pope had dreamed of launching the final crusade and enjoying eternal fame as the savior of the Holy Land. Gregory had literally driven the Emperor Frederick II to Palestine only to have that practical minded monarch conclude a ten-year truce with the enemies of Christ. But the pope was not discouraged. While with one hand he waged bitter war against the emperor in Italy, with the other he scattered legates over Europe to press the cross upon the barons of the land. Hence Gregory was ready to welcome with open arms any potent and hardy knight who might be persuaded to embrace the sacred cause. Despite his recent reverses Peter was one of the most prominent of French barons, and he was reputed to be a highly capable captain. During the summer of 1235 Thibaut of Champagne, Hugh of Burgundy, and Amaury of Montfort formally assumed the cross. Peter, however, was unwilling to commit himself to an expedition to the Holy Land until he had secured the future position of himself and his family. He apparently hinted to the pope that he would be ready to take the vows of a crusader as soon as he felt certain of the safety of his children and their lands. Gregory promptly demonstrated his eagerness to encourage the duke's good intentions. On October 13, 1235, he issued letters which placed John and Yolande of Brittany under

[2] *Registres de Grégoire IX,* nos. 2178, 2179.

the special protection of the Holy See. Because of his appreciation of their father's devotion to the church in her time of
need and the pious virtues of their mother, Gregory took them
under the sheltering wing of Rome until they should reach
their majority. Two Cistercian abbots were ordered to prevent
anyone from molesting the heirs of Brittany.[3] It must have
required some fairly definite indication of Peter's crusading
ardor to move the pope to praise his devotion to the church.
The duke had gained a mighty friend—the sole one who could
at once calm fulminating bishops and overawe angry kings.

While he was establishing his position as a favorite son of
the church, Peter was hard at work repairing his political fences
in France. If he were not to stand isolated at the complete
mercy of the royal government, he had to find new allies to
replace the counts of Boulogne and Dreux. Fortunately
another great vassal of the crown was in need of friends.
Thibaut of Champagne was beginning to feel that Blanche had
treated him rather shabbily. In the summer of 1234 the mediation of the queen and her son had enabled him to settle his
controversy with Alix of Cyprus, but the price had been extremely high. Alix received £40,000 of Tours in cash and
lands worth £2,000 a year. In order to raise the cash payment,
which slightly exceeded the net annual revenue of Champagne,
Thibaut was obliged to sell to King Louis his suzerainty over
the counties of Blois, Chartres, and Sancerre, and the viscounty
of Châteaudun.[4] As the barons who had brought Alix to
France and supported her claim to Champagne had been moved
primarily by a desire to punish Thibaut for assisting Blanche, it
seemed peculiarly unjust that Louis should take advantage of
the situation to purchase at a bargain price the four most
valuable fiefs held of the count. The king was a lover of
justice who was in due time to be hailed as a saint, but he

[3] *Ibid.*, nos. 2813, 2814. Aubri de Trois-Fontaines asserts that Peter assumed
the cross with Thibaut of Champagne, but this is almost certainly erroneus.
Monumenta Germaniae historica, Scriptores, XXIII, 937. Peter was first
designated as *crucesignatus* and given the privileges usually granted to crusaders
in papal letters of October 23, 1236. *Registres de Grégoire IX*, nos. 3363-3366.

[4] *Layettes*, II, nos. 2310, 2312. Jubainville, *Histoire des comtes de Champagne*, IV, 803.

could not permit gratitude to Thibaut to hamper the crown's efforts to weaken the great barons of France. The count of Champagne on his side was forced to nurse his grievances in silence for the death of his uncle called him to the Pyrenees to press his claim to the throne of Navarre. Not until the summer of 1235 was Thibaut firmly enough established in his new kingdom to be able to turn his attention to his interests in France. Then, however, he set to work to recover the fiefs which had been extorted from him. His first step was to look about for allies who would be willing to aid him against the king. On August 15, 1235, Peter and John of Brittany met King Thibaut at the latter's stronghold of Château-Thierry and agreed that if a papal dispensation could be obtained, John would marry Thibaut's daughter Blanche.[5]   As there was no chance whatever that Louis and his mother would consent to this alliance, Peter and Thibaut were in effect forming a new league against the crown. The king of Navarre soon announced that he had not sold the counties of Blois and Chartres to Louis but had merely pawned them, and he demanded the opportunity to redeem his pledges. Louis replied with perfect justice that the transaction had been a definite sale.[6]   Meanwhile Pope Gregory had hastened to oblige the crusader lord of Navarre by issuing a dispensation for the marriage of John and Blanche.[7]   The ceremony was performed at Château-Thierry on January 13, 1236. Thibaut gave Blanche as her marriage portion the suzerainty over the county of Perche and the right of succession to the kingdom of Navarre. Peter and John dowered her with one-third of Brittany and one-half of Peter's fiefs in France.[8]   The duke of Brittany had secured for himself the alliance of the most powerful baron of France and for his son a sound claim to the realm of Navarre which that canny young man was eventually to exchange for ready cash.

[5] *Thesaurus novus anecdotorum seu collectio monumentorum* (edd. E. Martène and U. Durand, Paris, 1717), I, 991.

[6] Aubri de Trois-Fontaines, *Monumenta Germaniae historica, Scriptores,* XXIII, 938. *Ménestrel de Reims,* p. 184. Joinville, p. 32.

[7] Jubainville, *Catalogue,* no. 2634.

[8] *Layettes,* II, no. 2432. Jubainville, *Catalogue,* nos. 2377-2411, 2454. Thibaut acquired the suzerainty over Perche through his mother. *Ibid.,* nos. 1699-1705.

The friendship of the count of Champagne assured Peter of support in the political arena of France, but there was another baron whose good will could be more directly useful to him. The duke's private interests demanded the fullest possible exploitation of his wife's claims in northern Poitou, and the real master of that region was the count of La Marche. The Duchess Margaret's first husband, Hugh of Thouars, had held the district of Aunis, and she claimed it as part of her dowry. But Hugh of Lusignan maintained that the Aunis belonged to him, and the dispute had been taken to the ecclesiastical courts where it had dragged on for over five years.[9] Peter decided that the time had come for a definite agreement with the powerful house of Lusignan. With its support he could defy with impunity the viscount of Thouars. In the early spring of 1236 he concluded a marriage alliance with the count of La Marche. The latter's son, Hugh of Lusignan the younger, was to marry Yolande of Brittany and to receive as her marriage portion the castellaries of Lamballe and Moncontour.[10] This was a shrewd stroke on Peter's part. These two castellaries were an important part of the lands which he had taken from Henry of Avagor. Henry had supported King Louis against the duke and was loudly demanding that the royal government should force Peter to restore his possessions. Louis might well aid his supporter against the conquered duke, but he would be certain to hesitate if his action would offend the mighty count of La Marche. This treaty with Hugh of Lusignan also included a settlement of the dispute over Aunis, but it is not clear what the arrangement was. The suzerainty was certainly given to the count of La Marche, but Peter and Margaret may have been in possession as his vassals.[11]

These two marriage alliances were a diplomatic triumph for Peter. Not only had he secured the friendship of two great barons of France, but he had also made it to their interest to

[9] *Layettes*, II, no. 1963. *Registres de Grégoire IX*, no. 2763.

[10] Morice, *Preuves*, I, 111.

[11] King Louis had given Aunis to Hugh in 1230, and the latter surrendered it to Alphonse of Poitou in 1241. *Layettes*, II, nos. 2052, 2928. I can find no evidence as to who was in actual possession of this fief during the years 1230-1241.

maintain his position in Brittany. Thibaut would be alert to defend Blanche's dowry and Hugh to guard Yolande's marriage portion. The duke's next step was to draw his two allies together. In April 1236 Hugh of Lusignan and his wife Isabel agreed that if anyone attacked the king of Navarre, they would support him in any way Peter might suggest.[12] As a matter of fact neither the duke of Brittany nor the count of La Marche were to be of much help to Thibaut for their lands lay far from the scene of the impending conflict. When he learned of the marriage of John and Blanche, Louis prepared for war. Thibaut on his side mustered his vassals and put his castles in a state of defense. But there was really no danger of hostilities. Thibaut could not face the royal host which advanced against him in early June, and Louis' enthusiasm was dampened by the mightiest of Peter's allies. The pope absolutely forbade the French king to attack the lands of Thibaut or any other crusader. While Gregory's letters must have arrived in France after the dispute had been settled, his attitude was undoubtedly well known to Louis. The pope had authorized the marriage in question, and it was his duty to protect all crusaders. The whole quarrel was amicably arranged. Thibaut renounced forever his claim to the suzerainty of Blois, Chartres, Sancerre, and Châteaudun and surrendered two castles to the king as temporary pledges of good behavior. He also paid the cost of Louis' military preparations.[18] The real victor was Peter. He had immeasurably strengthened his position and that of his children at no cost whatever to himself.

Last Blows at the Bretons

While he was achieving such decided success in his foreign relations, Peter was extremely hard pressed in his own duchy. In the summer of 1235 King Louis instituted a series of inquisitions to determine the extent of the injuries which Peter had inflicted on his vassals. One of these was a general investiga-

---

[12] *Layettes*, II, no. 2443. Mousket, II, 616-617.

[18] Aubri de Trois-Fontaines, *Monumenta Germaniae historica, Scriptores*, XXIII, 938. *Ménestrel de Reims*, pp. 183-185. Nangis, *Gesta, Historiens de France*, XX, 322-324. *Registres de Grégoire IX*, nos. 3195-3197.

tion to examine his violations of the established customs of Brittany. Others were held for the benefit of individual barons and ecclesiastical foundations.[14] They were not intended to be impartial in their procedure. The general inquisition drew its witnesses from the vassals of the house of Léon and of Henry of Avagor, both bitter enemies of the duke. In the cases of the investigations for individuals the witnesses were apparently chosen by the plaintiffs. Nevertheless the testimony as a whole inspires one with confidence in its essential accuracy. Where the facts stated can be controlled from other sources, they are found to be correct. The witnesses were careful to state when they spoke from direct knowledge and when from hearsay, and they often pleaded ignorance. In short it would seem that the inquests were not essentially unfair to the duke, but they must have been extremely embarrassing to him. They reviewed his relations with his barons from the early days of his reign when he changed the customs of Brittany in his own favor and despoiled the lords of Léon and Henry of Avagor to his violations of the truces of 1231 and 1234. When he married Alix, Peter had promised Philip Augustus that he would deprive his barons of neither lands nor privileges. In concluding the truces with Louis IX he had sworn to do no harm to those of his vassals who had aided the king against him. The inquisitions made it perfectly clear that he had observed none of these promises.

The fact that Louis saw fit to hold these inquests implied that he intended to force the duke to abandon his unjustified claims and to make restitution to those whom he had damaged. But this would have been entirely impracticable. Although Peter in his act of submission had stated that he placed himself completely at the king's mercy, that was simply a pleasant form. In reality the relations between the crown and the duke of Brittany were bound to rest on mutual compromise. Louis had twice given Peter his fill of actual warfare, but he had never conquered Brittany. While it would be reckless to assert that the resources of the French crown were insufficient to enable

[14] *Nouveau recueil*, pp. 97-134. *Layettes*, I, no. 1061; II, nos. 2417-2419. See Painter, "Documents on the history of Brittany," *Speculum*, XI (1936), 470-472.

the king to reduce the duchy completely, such an enterprise would have been long, difficult, and enormously expensive. Louis' invasions of Peter's lands had merely involved the border lordships—the real Brittany stood behind untouched and well-nigh impregnable. The king had besieged St. Aubin, but he had never even threatened Sucinio. King Louis had only one means of coercing Peter—he could retain the three castles which the duke had surrendered as a guarantee that he would treat his vassals as the king should direct. But Peter was not likely to worry very much about what might happen at Easter 1238. By that time John would be duke of Brittany and Peter a sworn crusader. In short it is extremely improbable that Louis when he inaugurated the inquests had any real expectation that he could enforce their findings. It is certain that Henry of Avagor neither recovered his lost lands nor received compensation for the damages which he had suffered during the truce.[15] While the witnesses at the inquests carefully evaluated the injuries which Peter had inflicted on the lord of Combourg and the bishop of Dol, there is no evidence that the duke ever attempted to pay these claims.[16] King Louis' closest ally, André of Vitré, obtained a settlement of some of his demands, but most of the damage which he had suffered was made good by the king instead of by Peter. The duke did agree that neither he nor his successors would claim the rights of relief and wardship over the baronies of Vitré, Fougères, Combourg, and Acigné, but the fact that this was the subject of a special concession indicates that Peter did not abandon these disputed prerogatives in the rest of the duchy.[17] While the inquisitions were undoubtedly a severe humiliation to the duke of Brittany, it is extremely unlikely that they actually weakened his authority. Peter undoubtedly owed his success in escaping the full possible consequences of his defeat principally to the essential strength of his position as duke of Brittany. Nevertheless it is important to remember that a new hand was grasping the reins of government in France. King Louis was of age, and Blanche of Castille was no longer the absolute mistress of the royal policy.

[15] *Querimonia Henrici de Avaugor, Historiens de France*, XXIV, 729-731.
[16] *Nouveau recueil*, pp. 122-128, 131-134.
[17] *Layettes*, II, no. 2447. *Recueil*, nos. 108-109.

The queen regent had been Peter's bitter foe, but there is reason for believing that young Louis both liked and admired the energetic and colorful duke of Brittany.[18]

The baronial opposition to Peter's policy had made little headway—the prelates of the duchy were no more successful. The reader will recall that the duke, supported by his vassals assembled at Redon, had formally defied the church and driven the protesting bishops into exile. But even Peter felt unequal to fighting the church and the crown at once. As soon as he had definitely committed himself to the alliance with England, he took steps toward reconciliation with Rome. In January 1230 he dispatched an agent to the papal court and gave him full authority to make terms with the pope and the Breton bishops. Early in the following summer the duke ratified an agreement which involved a complete surrender to the church. The decisions of the council of Redon were declared void, and Peter promised to make good any damage he had done to church property.[19] The bishops of Brittany returned to the duchy and lived at peace with the duke—for several months.

Duke Peter did not again attempt a general assault on the church's position, but confined himself to a series of fierce disputes with individual bishops. He seized the town of St. Malo which belonged to the bishop and chapter of that see, and when the churchmen protested, he drove them out of the duchy.[20] He quarrelled with the bishop of Rennes over ecclesiastical property which had been occupied by the fortifications of the city.[21] When the bishop of Tréguier excommunicated a group of knights who had committed outrages against the clergy and people of his episcopal city, the duke refused to compel the culprits to submit to the church.[22] The bishops of Vannes, Dol, and St. Brieuc soon came to the aid of their harassed colleagues, and a fresh cloud of excommunications and interdicts fell on

---

[18] I base this belief largely on Joinville who clearly admired Peter and seems to imply that the king also did.

[19] Morice, *Preuves*, I, 909-910. *Registres de Grégoire IX*, nos. 464, 465.

[20] *Ibid.*, nos. 1975, 2191.

[21] *Ibid.*, no. 2192.

[22] *Ibid.*, nos. 757, 1703, 1765, 1976, 2158.

Peter and his duchy.²³ Free use of the ever-reliable appeal to
Rome enabled the duke to delay the proceedings against him,
but late in the summer of 1234 his desire to court papal favor
prompted him to offer to appear in person before Gregory's
court to answer the charges of the Breton prelates. The pope
promptly suspended the various sentences which had been
launched against Peter, and this truce was prolonged indefinitely by Gregory's anxiety to persuade the duke to participate
in the coming crusade. When the latter finally assumed the
cross in 1236, he received papal letters which forbade any excommunication to be launched against him without the pope's
approval.²⁴ Peter neither went to Rome nor gave any satisfaction to his bishops. While Gregory continued to dispatch letters of admonition, they were decidedly lacking in sharpness
and were cheerfully ignored.²⁵

Although the last years of Peter's reign as duke of Brittany
were a period of comparative calm in his relations with most
of his clergy, it was marked by an unusually violent quarrel
with the church of Nantes. During the years 1230-1234 the
duke had waged continuous war on the temporal authority of
Henry, bishop of Nantes. He arrested and executed criminals
on the bishop's lands despite the latter's right to high justice,
and he plagued the bishop's merchants with special taxes. Excommunications and interdicts were of no effect. Then when
Bishop Henry died late in 1234, Peter set to work to loot the
diocese. His agents seized the church's tithes and levied aids
from the late bishop's men. The bishop's houses were stripped
of doors and windows, his fish-ponds denuded of fish, and his
woods cut down and sold. When the complaints of the local
clergy brought forth a protest from Rome, the duke answered
it by destroying vineyards and salt works belonging to the
bishop's men. Peter's exactions were estimated at over £6,000
and the value of the property which he destroyed at £7,000.
On December 3, 1236, Gregory ordered a commission headed
by the bishop of Poitiers to compel Peter to make restitution,

---

²³ *Ibid.*, no. 2178.

²⁴ *Ibid.*, nos. 2178, 2190, 3363-3366.

²⁵ *Ibid.*, nos. 3988, 4047. On these quarrels see Haut-Jussé, *Les papes et les
ducs de Bretagne*, I, 87-91, 104-107.

but as the duke was a crusader who had been granted exemption from excommunication or interdict at the hands of anyone except the pope himself, this body could take no decisive action.[26] Peter, of course, had no reason for wishing to make peace. His reign as duke of Brittany was nearly over, and he had no intention of disgorging any of his booty or making any agreements which might hamper his successor.

Duke Peter passed into the pages of history under the cognomen *Malusclericus* which may be roughly rendered as "the plague of the clerks." [27] Few men have so richly deserved their nicknames. Except for the momentary reconciliations of 1221 and 1230, he was perpetually at odds with all the prelates of Brittany but one—his chancellor and close ally the bishop of Quimper. When he could not avoid them by appeals to Rome, he took excommunications and interdicts in his stride. But one must not forget that the issues in these controversies were essentially political. Peter had resolved to reduce the independence of his vassals both lay and ecclesiastical, and he pursued that end with relentless energy and determination. If the king of France chose to support the barons of Brittany and the pope the bishops, the duke was willing to defy them both. This indifference to excommunications does not, however, prove that Peter was irreligious. While one hand threatened the bishops, the other distributed largesse to various ecclesiastical foundations. Peter was neither saint nor demon—his behavior was entirely conventional for a baron of his day. His uniqueness as a nemesis of the clergy lay in the thoroughness with which he carried out his policy. Most barons were content with a puttering squabble with the local bishop balanced by small pious donations. Peter drove six bishops from their dioceses and went on four crusades against heretics and infidels. The southern rose window of Chartres glows with the fame of the scourge of the clergy—Peter *Malusclericus*.

In November 1237 John of Brittany reached his twenty-first birthday, and the most important phase of Peter's career came

---

[26] Morice, *Preuves*, I, 903, 935-939. *Registres de Grégoire IX*, no. 3387.

[27] The best discussion of the origin of this cognomen is in Haut-Jussé, *Les papes et les ducs de Bretagne*, I, 48-49.

to an end.[28]   Peter, duke of Brittany and earl of Richmond, became Peter of Braine, knight.[29]   Although he lived for thirteen years after his son's accession, his place in history depends on his reign as duke of Brittany.   Unfortunately in recent years his reputation has fallen prey to French and Breton nationalists. M. Élie Berger saw in him only the rebellious baron who dared to interfere with the divinely ordained destiny of the house of Capet.   The foe of Blanche of Castille was to him the enemy of France.   M. de la Borderie on the other hand disliked Peter as a Frenchman who had robbed the princes of true Breton blood of their inheritance.   He usurped both wife and duchy from Henry of Avagor.   Both these viewpoints are essentially unhistorical.   Peter was a feudal baron whose duty was to care for his family and its possessions.   When he married Alix of Thouars, he undertook to protect and if possible augment her inheritance and deliver it to his and her heirs.   One must be careful not to allow Peter's colorful and unfortunate adventures in the French political arena to obscure his real success as duke of Brittany.   He made decided reductions in the privileges of both the prelates and barons of the duchy and established precedents which were to be highly useful to his successors.   By his efforts the counts of Léon and Tréguier were reduced to the status of ordinary vassals.   The regalian rights over the sees of St. Pol, Tréguier, and St. Brieuc were secured for the duke, and all of the counties of Tréguier and Lamballe except the Goëllo district was annexed to his demesne.   The new castles of St. Aubin and Gâvre watched over the great lords of the Breton marches.   Peter did not succeed in creating a feudal state as advanced as Flanders or Champagne, but he made an excellent beginning.   He left John and Yolande united by marriage to powerful baronial houses of France and in full enjoyment of an augmented inheritance.

If a son's emulation of his father is a mark of the latter's success as a parent, Peter attained the summit of paternal perfection.   As soon as he succeeded to the duchy, John plunged into war with his barons and gaily took up his father's quarrels

---

[28] *Cartulaire de Vitré*, no. 399.

[29] He used this title on February 11, 1238.   René Blanchard, "Cartulaire des sires de Rays," *Archives historiques du Poitou*, XXX (1899), 184.

with the church. He resolutely maintained his father's usurpations and committed new ones himself. Peter's lack of scruple,
his invincible determination, and his affection for hard cash
were all found in his son. In fact the two men were not only
alike in character, but they seem to have been in perfect accord
with one another. During the years 1230-1234 when royal
hosts were periodically invading Brittany because of Peter's
political activities, John was old enough to have opinions of his
own. If he had disapproved of his father's policies, he could
easily have joined the Breton rebels in their support of King
Louis. While he might not have gained a free hand in Brittany,
he could probably have obtained a new guardian. His continuous cooperation with Peter during those difficult years seems
proof of their mutual understanding.

Had Peter been asked to estimate his success as duke of Brittany, he would have boasted of the accomplishments mentioned
above. He had increased the ducal authority and had left a
son competent to carry on his work. The historian, however,
must form a still higher estimate of the significance of his reign.
Peter and John ruled Brittany in a period when the political
institutions of France were changing rapidly. The governmental powers which had been highly dispersed under the purely
feudal organization of society were being concentrated more
and more in the hands of a few potentates. If a great baron
of France succeeded in holding his own against the encroach-
ments of the crown, the general trend of the time tended to make
him a semi-independent sovereign loosely allied to the French
king. If he failed to maintain his rights, the same forces reduced him to the position of a more or less highly privileged
subject. Two less capable and vigorous dukes might have seen
Brittany absorbed into the royal demesne as Normandy had
been. The duchy owed in large measure her long and proud
history as an independent state bound to the French crown by
the loosest of feudal ties to her first two dukes of the house of
Dreux.

Prospective Crusader

The accession of John to the duchy of Brittany reduced
Peter's possessions to his share of the lands of the house of

Dreux and the fiefs which he had acquired during his stormy career. The former consisted of the castles of Brie-Comte-Robert and Fère-en-Tardenois with their appurtenances and two manors to the southwest of Paris. They were held as fiefs from Peter's nephew, John, count of Dreux.[30] These small domains on the borders of the Ile-de-France yielded a revenue and were useful as occasional residences, but they were of little strategic value to a baron whose interests lay in the west. The treaty of peace with Louis in November 1234 had deprived Peter of the most valuable of his acquisitions—St. James, Bellême, and La Perrière. As he was also forced to renounce all claims to the lands in Anjou and Maine which he had held under the treaty of Vendôme, any ambition he may have cherished to build up a strong territorial position in that region had been completely frustrated. Of all his personal acquisitions the treaty of 1234 left him only the Angevin barony which he had taken from Thibaut Crespin with its castles of Champtoceaux and Mont-faucon. Fortunately the latter stronghold was ideally situated for cooperation with the fortresses of the lands which Peter enjoyed by right of his second wife, Margaret of Montaigu. Montfaucon stood in the southwestern corner of Anjou, and only a narrow salient from the Breton barony of Clisson separated it from the lordship of Montaigu. The baronies of La Garnache and Montaigu formed a compact fief which comprised the northwestern part of the viscounty of Thouars. If Peter hoped to continue to be of importance in feudal politics, his opportunity lay in this region where Poitou, Anjou, and Brittany met.

Despite his preoccupation during the years 1235-1237 with his duties as duke of Brittany and father of John and Yolande, Peter had not neglected his personal interests. His principal concern was undoubtedly to replace the revenues which he had lost by the treaty of 1234 and to increase his territorial power, but these were not the only considerations. Somewhere along Peter's chequered course he had found relief from war and politics in a lady named Nicole who bore him an illegitimate

[30] *Cartulaire de Notre-Dame de Paris*, II, 262. *Layettes*, II, no. 1720. *Gallia Christiana*, VII, 863. Morice, *Preuves*, I, 898.

son, Oliver.[31]   Now Peter had no lands with which he could endow this boy.   When Margaret of Montaigu died, her baronies would pass to her kinsman Maurice of Belleville[32]   While Peter did succeed in holding La Garnache and Montaigu as long as he lived, he could not give them to his bastard.[33]   Half of his fiefs in France had been granted in dower to John's wife Blanche of Champagne, and apparently the other half formed part of the marriage portion of Yolande.[34]   If Oliver were to be supported as befitted his father's rank, Peter would have to acquire a new fief.

In the year 1235 fortune favored this laudable ambition. More than half of the part of the duchy of Brittany which lay south of the Loire was included in the great barony of Retz. Late in the twelfth century Ralph I of Retz had given the southern part of his fief, the lordship of Machecoul, as an appanage to a younger son.   The lands of the lord of Machecoul were adjacent to the Poitevin baronies of La Garnache and Montaigu and hence ideally situated for Peter.   In 1235 Beatrice, lady of Machecoul and of La Roche-sur-Yon and Lucon in Poitou, died leaving an infant daughter in the care of her husband, Aimery of Thouars, the second son of the Viscount Aimery VII.[35] Coolly ignoring the rights of the lord of Retz who was the immediate suzerain of Machecoul, Peter seized the fief.[36]   He apparently tried to gain possession of La Roche-sur-Yon as well, but there he was foiled by King Louis who seized that fortress and Lucon.[37]   When the young Jeanne of Machecoul

[31] For a discussion of Oliver see appendix III.

[32] Maurice, lord of Commequiers, was the heir male of the house of Montaigu. Louis de la Boutetière, "Dons d'hommes au xiii° siècle en Bas-Poitou," *Archives historiques du Poitou*, I (1872), 89-91, 111.   In 1205 Margaret was called *heres legitima Montis Acuti* (*ibid.*, pp. 81-82), but no one has been able to place her convincingly in the family genealogy.   See appendix II.

[33] Morice, *Preuves*, I, 915, 924, 930.

[34] *Ibid.*, column 898. *Gallia Christiana*, VII, 864.

[35] "Cartulaire de Rays," *Archives historiques du Poitou*, XXX (1899), 30, 101.

[36] *Ibid.*, XXVIII (1898), cxxix.

[37] Peter's attack on La Roche-sur-Yon is mentioned in a papal letter of 1248 as having taken place about this time.   Morice, *Preuves*, I, 936.   See also above Chapter I, note 28.   At the inquests held in Poitou in 1247 the chaplain

married, she recovered La Roche-sur-Yon and Lucon, but Peter kept a firm hold on Machecoul even after his retirement as duke of Brittany.[38] In 1239 his wife, Margaret, used the titles of lady of La Garnache, Montaigu, and Machecoul.[39] There seems no possible way of justifying Peter's action. His rather doubtful right to the custody of Machecoul came to an end when Jeanne married, and it belonged to the duke of Brittany not to Peter of Braine. Peter's retention of the fief was a pure usurpation which must have been acquiesced in by his son John. It was this lordship of Machecoul that Peter intended to leave to his son Oliver.[40] There could be no more appropriate arrangement—a fief obtained illegally for an illegitimate son.

When Peter lost the duchy of Brittany, he retired to his domains to the south of the Loire. He was the dominant power in the coastal region between Nantes and La Rochelle. To the north of his lands lay those of his son while to the south stood the castles of his friend and ally Hugh of Lusignan. In theory Peter held La Garnache and Montaigu as a vassal of the viscount of Thouars, but that lord found himself utterly unable to enforce his rights as suzerain. Peter continued to hold the castle of Mareuil-sur-Lay which properly belonged to the viscount's demesne and completely ignored his feudal obligations to the viscount. The Viscount Guy of Thouars appealed to the pope and later to Alphonse, count of Poitou,

of Copechagnière which lay near La Roche-sur-Yon complained that his church had been burned by a royal army *cum ultima guerra fuit inter dominum regem Francie et dominum P. Montis acuti. Archives historiques du Poitou*, XXV (1895), 324. I believe this refers to the same affair.

[38] *Layettes*, III, no. 3628. This document is a complaint addressed by Guy, viscount of Thouars, to Alphonse, count of Poitou. He complains that the seneschal of Poitou, Hardouin of Maillé, first husband of Jeanne, refused him homage for La Roche-sur-Yon and Lucon. This letter must be dated between 1241 when Alphonse became count of Poitou and April 1242 when Guy had been succeeded by his brother Aimery VIII. *Ibid.*, II, no. 2972. The editor of the *Layettes* places Guy's death in 1247, but he has confused the accession of his brother, Aimery VIII, with that of his son, Aimery IX.

[39] "Cartulaire de Rays," *Archives historiques du Poitou*, XXVIII (1898), cxxix.

[40] *Ibid.*, p. cxxxii; XXX (1899), 254-256.

but all to no avail.[41] Peter went on his way ruling his broad lands from his castle of La Garnache.[42]

Peter of Braine could not, however, settle down to enjoy peaceful domesticity in La Vendée—a fact which was undoubtedly a source of satisfaction both to himself and to his neighbors. Late in the summer of 1236 he had formally and definitely assumed the cross.[43] The Latin empire of Constantinople was in desperate straits, and the pope was urging the chivalry of Europe to go to its assistance. He offered the command of the projected expedition to Peter.[44] This magnificent opportunity quickly warmed the duke's crusading fervor. While he had not been able to view with any great enthusiasm the prospect of journeying to the Holy Land in a subordinate capacity, the idea of leading an expedition of his own appealed to him immensely. He made only one stipulation—he should not be obliged to obey any commands of the emperor, the patriarch, or the doge of Venice if they seemed to him to be unwise.[45] By December 1237 the following June 24 had been set as the date for the departure of the expedition. Peter suggested to the pope that he should lead a force of 2,000 horsemen and 10,000 infantry. Since the authorities at Constantinople apparently considered this army too large, Gregory asked Peter to content himself with 1,500 horse and 6,000 foot.[46] Crusading plans must never be taken too seriously. The expedition did not start until the summer of 1239, and Peter went to Acre instead of to Constantinople.

The extremely ambitious scale of Peter's project forces one to pose a most interesting question—where was the necessary money coming from? Even if the 1,500 cavalry and 6,000 infantry were all volunteers who supplied their own equipment and served without pay, their transportation and maintenance

[41] *Layettes,* III, no. 3628, and note 38 above. *Registres de Grégoire IX,* nos. 2819, 3225, 4039.

[42] La Garnache was Peter's chief seat after his resignation of the duchy of Brittany. Morice, *Preuves,* I, 924.

[43] *Registres de Grégoire IX,* nos. 3363-3366.

[44] Matthew Paris, *Chronica maiora* (ed. H. R. Luard, *Rolls series*), III, 387. Mousket, II, 630.

[45] *Registres de Grégoire IX,* no. 3363.

[46] *Ibid.,* nos. 4012, 4027.

would be very costly. Since it seems clear that some at least of Peter's troops were to be mercenaries, the cost of the expedition would be enormous.[47] Crusades were by far the most expensive form of recreation known to feudal barons. Peter's younger brother, Count John of Macon, sold his county to King Louis in order to raise money to support his contingent in this crusade.[48] But Peter was no reckless enthusiast who would spend his treasure and sell his lands for God's cause. He had in all probability a good reserve of ready cash. As late as 1249-1250 he was able to lend King Louis £8,000.[49] Nevertheless he showed no inclination to use his own funds. He was going to Constantinople at the pope's behest, and Gregory could find him the necessary money. The pope did his best. Good catholics were encouraged to make gifts and legacies for the crusade, and those who had taken the cross and found themselves unable to carry out their vows were allowed to buy their release with a suitable contribution. All the money collected from these sources in the provinces of Rouen and Tours and the diocese of Poitiers was assigned to Peter. He was to receive one-third at once and the remaining two-thirds after he reached Constantinople.[50] Apparently, however, there was difficulty in collecting the money.[51] It is quite possible that the clergy had little enthusiasm for raising funds for Peter, their bitter foe, and that the relief of Constantinople did not appeal to the faithful as did a crusade to the Holy Land. No definite figures are available, but the most plausible explanation of Peter's abandonment of his plan to conduct an independent expedition is that he could not obtain enough money to support it. When he finally changed his objective from Constantinople to the Holy Land and sailed for Acre with King Thibaut, he surrendered in favor of the Emperor Baldwin his claim to the funds raised by the church for his expedition to aid the Latin empire.[52] It is impossible to say whether or not Peter had

[47] *Ibid.*, no. 4028.
[48] *Layettes*, II, no. 2776.
[49] *Gallia Christiana*, VII, *Instrumenta*, p. 280.
[50] *Registres de Grégoire IX*, nos. 4025, 4026, 4265, 4266, 4316, 5305.
[51] *Ibid.*, no. 4527.
[52] *Ibid.*, no. 5305.

already pocketed his one-third of the collection. One can merely state that as he was able to loan as large a sum as £8,000 in 1249, he could not have spent much of his own money on his crusade.

Before Peter could set out on his pious adventure, there were a few matters to be settled with King Louis. Although the treaty of 1234 had provided for the return of the charters by which the king had granted to the duke of Brittany the castles of St. James and Bellême, Peter had failed to produce these documents. He asserted that he could not find them, but Louis refused to believe him. In April 1238 Peter and his son appeared before the king at Pontoise and issued solemn letters promising that they would search for the charters and return them if they could be found. In any case the documents were to be considered void.[53] One is compelled to share Louis' doubt about the loss of these royal letters. Feudal barons were unlikely to mislay documents which proved their rights to valuable fiefs. It is probable that Peter hoped that he or his heirs might some day find the charters useful in bargaining with the crown. Thibaut of Champagne had given his suzerainty over the county of Perche to John of Brittany, and Bellême was the chief seat of the counts of Perche.[54] His suzerainty and his charter might enable John eventually to recover the castle and fief. While it is sad to find a diplomatist of Peter's capacity and imagination grasping at such feeble straws, one cannot but admire his persistence. His record for calm disregard of his most solemn promises was kept unsullied to the end.

In June 1239 Peter made his final arrangements with King Louis. Margaret of Montaigu had long enjoyed a royal pension of £200 from the revenues of La Rochelle. While it had been granted specifically to Margaret for her lifetime, Louis knew Peter's capacity for concocting ingenious claims and insisted that he formally agree that the pension should revert to the crown at Margaret's death. At the same time Peter surrendered to the king his castle of Champtoceaux to hold until

[53] Morice, *Preuves*, I, 906-907. *Layettes*, II, no. 2705.
[54] Jubainville, *Catalogue*, no. 2454.

a year after his return from the crusade. If he died on the expedition, Louis would turn the castle over to his heir a year after the other crusaders reached France. In case Peter was detained in prison by Saracen or Greek, the king would dispose of Champtoceaux·as he might direct by trusty messenger. Should Peter commit any offense against Louis, the latter could hold the castle until the question had been settled by the royal court.[55] The king clearly had a high opinion of his vassal's capacity for mischief and intended to retain some hold over him. As the church would not allow an attack on the lands of crusaders, Louis demanded Champtoceaux as a pledge for Peter's good behavior.

Few barons who bore the cross can have looked forward to the performance of their crusading vows as serenely as Peter. He had no cause for regret at leaving home. For one who as duke of Brittany had ruled a great fief and had played an important part in the politics of France and England, life as lord of Montaigu must have been exceedingly dull. His wife was at least fifty years old and probably an invalid. His lands were sheltered by the might of Rome and watched over from the north and from the south by the strongholds of his son John and his ally Hugh of Lusignan. The viscount of Thouars, his sole enemy of any importance, could not defy Rome, Brittany, and La Marche. Then Peter was in the vicinity of his fiftieth year, and it behooved him to consider the state of his soul. A feudal God could perhaps overlook the habitual violation of most solemn oaths and the continuous instigation of war and rapine, but He could hardly fail to resent the oppression of His clergy. Throughout his life Peter had treated the fulminations of the successors of the Apostles with an indifference which sprang not from disbelief but from the knowledge that when the time came he could easily secure forgiveness for his derelictions. As a crusader received a plenary indulgence for all sins which he had duly confessed, Peter felt that he was clearing from his soul the varied debris of his turbulent career. Hence he could look forward with unalloyed pleasure to a long, adventurous journey, opportunities for glorious deeds of prowess, and days

[55] *Layettes*, II, nos. 1963, 2808, 2844.

and nights of camp life with gay companions. True his failure to raise sufficient money meant that he must lead a far more modest contingent than he had expected, and he would have to join forces with either the Emperor Baldwin or King Thibaut, but that probably did not worry him much. Constantinople or Acre could be equally entertaining. Certainly one could not seek a more diverting colleague than Thibaut *le Chansonnier*.

V

PLENARY INDULGENCE

Crusading Chief

The crusade of 1239-1240 was a joint enterprise of the houses of Capet, Dreux, and Champagne. King Louis, moved by a combination of religious ardor and desire to see Peter and Thibaut far from France, contributed a strong contingent of troops under the command of the chief military officer of the crown, Amaury, count of Montfort and constable of France.[1] Count Amaury was a professional crusader who had spent his life and his family fortune fighting the Albigensian heretics. In 1239 he was a noted soldier and a pauper—a brave, reckless baron devoted to the service of king and pope. He alone of the leaders of this crusade was a true successor of Godfrey of Bouillon and his paladins. Amaury's two colleagues were far less suited to their rôle. While Peter had a due regard for his spiritual balance sheet, it is unlikely that he was consumed with desire to rescue the Holy Land from the infidel. A crusade also offered unique opportunities to win the fame and glory which were sought by all chivalrous knights, but there is no evidence that Peter was devoted to the ideals of chivalry. In the absence of any indication that he was a patron and frequenter of tourneys as his father Count Robert II had been, one must assume that he had no particular enthusiasm for knightly deeds. Peter enjoyed a good fight—when the chances for profit seemed promising. If he gained his plenary indulgence and had a skirmish or two with the Turks, Peter's crusade would satisfy him completely. King Thibaut's ambitions were even more modest. Before leaving France the *Chansonnier* deluged the land with poems which explained why he had turned crusader.[2] Knights who refused to take the

[1] Aubri de Trois-Fontaines, *Monumenta Germaniae historica, Scriptores,* XXIII, 946.

[2] *Les chansons de croisade* (ed. Joseph Bédier, Paris, 1909), nos. 15-17.

cross were almost certain to go to hell and could hardly expect to enjoy much esteem while they lived. " Blind is the man who does not once in his life lend succor to God and for so little loses the praise of the world." A clear passage to heaven and a reputation as a man of worth and valor were what Thibaut sought.[3] But even within the limits set by his motives Thibaut could not be called an enthusiastic crusader. In a poem of farewell to his lady he asks " God! Why have you made the land beyond the sea which will separate so many lovers." He goes on to suggest that God certainly owes him a magnificent reward for taking so much trouble for His cause.[4] In short Thibaut felt that since the confounded Holy Land was there, it was necessary to make one crusade to assure future bliss and present popular esteem. He was no warrior but a composer of pleasant songs. Such were the three barons who were to govern the destinies of the crusading host.

The army embarked at Marseilles and set sail for Acre. Unfortunately the winds seemed to prefer Mahomet to Christ. As the fleet came within two days sail of its destination, a storm arose which dispersed it to the most distant shores of the Mediterranean. Eventually the ships found their way back to their course, and early in September 1239 the crusaders reached Acre.[5] As soon as they had established their camp on shore, the crusading barons met in council to elect a commander-in-chief and to agree on a plan of campaign. After a long debate they decided to move down the coast and to fortify the town of Ascalon in preparation for an attack on Damascus. There can have been no real question as to whom to choose as their chief. No king could be expected to serve under one of lesser rank. Hence Thibaut was promptly elected *caput et ductor* of the host, and all the crusaders vowed to obey

[3] *Ibid.*, no. 15, especially lines 1-4 and 19-21.

[4] *Ibid.*, no. 17, especially lines 5-8 and 25-32.

[5] *Le livre d'Eracles*, Rothelin manuscript, *Recueil des historiens des croisades, Historiens Occidentaux*, II, 529. This chronicle will be referred to as *Rothelin Eracles. Annales de Terre Sainte, Archives de l'Orient Latin*, II, 440. For a general account of this crusade see Reinhold Röhricht, " Die Kreuzzuge des Grafen Theobald von Navarra und Richard von Cornwallis nach dem heiligen Lande," *Forschungen zur deutschen Geschichte*, XXVI (1886), 69-81.

his orders.[6] This was little more than a pleasant formality
for nothing under heaven could curb the sublime individualism
of feudal barons. A king of France or England who could
seize the fiefs of the disobedient, or a legate who could con-
demn their souls could make some pretense of ruling a crusading army, but the king of Navarre was bound to be a mere
figurehead. Even the chroniclers who mention Thibaut's
election continue to assume that he and Peter were joint leaders.
Had the latter chosen to set an example of scrupulous obedience
to King Thibaut's orders, some discipline might have been
maintained in the army, but Peter was to be the first to allow
a personal whim to lead him into independent action.

No one could charge the leader of this crusade with undue
haste. For two whole months the army lay peacefully at Acre
before commencing its march toward Ascalon. The count' of
Montfort and the poor knights who had mortgaged all they
possessed for a chance to fight the infidel might fret and fume
at the delay, but Thibaut was in no hurry.[7] He was a crusader
because it was fashionable. Since Acre was in the Holy Land,
he saw no point in rushing off to seek Turks. Instead he composed plaintive songs to tell his lady what hardships he was
undergoing for the sake of Christ.[8] Even Peter who was no
ardent crusader must have grown impatient—he at least had
the instincts of a soldier. Be that as it may, it was November
1 before the army set out from Acre. Some ten days later it
pitched camp near Jaffa. There appear to have been in the
host about four thousand knights over half of whom belonged
to the contingents supplied by the barons of the kingdom of
Jerusalem. Like most crusading armies they were desperately
short of horses and provisions.[9] Hence when Peter learned
one day that a large convoy of edible animals bound for the
Turkish stronghold of Damascus was passing within striking
distance of his camp at Jaffa, he was sorely tempted to try to

[6] Nangis, *Chronicon*, I, 189. *Historiens de France*, XXIII, 110. *Rothelin Eracles*, p. 538.

[7] *Chansons de croisade*, no. 20, lines 3-7; no. 21, lines 31-40.

[8] *Ibid.*, no. 18.

[9] Aubri de Trois-Fontaines, *Monumenta Germaniae historica, Scriptores*, XXIII, 946. *Rothelin Eracles*, pp. 531-532.

intercept it. As he was unwilling to waste valuable time in debate with the cautious King Thibaut and far from anxious to share any booty to be gained, Peter decided to act independently with his own contingent. Late one evening he left the camp with a force of two hundred knights and mounted serjeants. The only man of baronial rank known to have been in the party was the noted trouvère Ralph de Nesle, a younger brother of Count John of Soissons, who had journeyed to Palestine as a member of Peter's military household. While it seems likely that André of Vitré, Ralph of Fougères, Guiomar of Léon, Henry of Avagor, and the other Bretons who took part in this crusade followed the banner of their former duke in this raid from Jaffa, the chronicler neglected to record their names. At dawn Peter and his men reached the castle in which the convoy had spent the night. Since there were two possible routes which the Turks could take on their way to Damascus, Peter divided his small army. One division under Ralph de Nesle was placed in ambush on one road while the count himself with the rest of the troop watched the other. At sunrise the Turks left their stronghold and started along the path held by Peter's party. When their leader found himself faced with a force inferior to his own, he decided to give battle rather than risk the loss of his convoy by retiring to the castle where he had spent the night. Peter had chosen his ground well. The greatest asset of the Turks in their battles with the crusaders was the speed with which their lightly-armed horsemen could maneuver. If they had plenty of space, they could easily avoid the lumbering charge and ferocious hand-to-hand combat which were the tactical mainstays of the European warriors. Peter had taken his stand just beyond a place where the road passed through a narrow defile in which his heavy cavalry would have an enormous advantage. In the hope of holding off the crusaders until he could get his convoy past this dangerous spot the Turkish leader sent forward his archers to attack Peter's men. But the French knights charged with such vigor that they drove the archers back on the main Turkish force before it could clear the defile. Then Peter and his followers went to work earnestly with sword and mace. Although the Turks were caught in a place where they could not escape from their heavily-armed opponents and were seriously hampered by the animals they were guarding, they fought so well that the outcome of the battle was long in doubt. In fact the crusaders might well have been defeated had not Peter sounded his horn to call in his other division. The arrival of Ralph de Nesle with his fresh troops was decisive. The Turks deserted their animals and escaped as best they could to the castle. As soon as Peter had collected his prisoners and booty, he returned triumphantly to Jaffa.[10]

Peter's raid was not only a worthy knightly exploit which brought the army desperately needed provisions, but it was to be the sole military triumph of the whole crusade. Unfortunately it is impossible to say with any certainty whether its success was the result of Peter's skill as a captain or of blind luck. If Peter had definite and reasonably reliable information as to the strength of the Turkish party, his plan of campaign was soundly conceived and ably executed. If on the other hand he lacked this knowledge, the raid was a reckless adventure and the division of his small force into two parties pure insanity. As Peter's career in general shows no tendency on his part to engage in hazardous and uncertain enterprises where much was at stake for small possible gain, I am inclined to believe that he knew what he was about in this raid from Jaffa. In that case he showed himself a highly competent tactician. But this expedition which demonstrated Peter's worth as a captain made clear his utter lack of comprehension of the obligations incumbent on one of the leaders of a joint enterprise. His independent action without the knowledge of the chosen commander of the host set a bad example for his fellow barons. Worse yet his success filled them with envy. The counts of Montfort and Bar and the duke of Burgundy promptly decided to win some renown for themselves. A strong Turkish force was known to be at Gaza which lay some distance beyond Ascalon. The three barons planned to leave Jaffa ahead of the main body of the army, attack the enemy at Gaza, and rejoin the host at Ascalon. Thibaut, Peter, and the

---

[10] The fullest and most circumstantial account of Peter's raid is in the *Rothelin Eracles*, pp. 533-536. The stories contained in the other chronicles seem based on letters such as that in Matthew Paris, *Chronica maiora*, IV, 25.

masters of the Templars and the Hospitallers tried to dissuade them. King Thibaut recalled the oaths of obedience they had sworn when they chose him leader at Acre. No argument had any effect. Amaury of Montfort, constable of France and lifelong captain in the service of the Holy Church, was the idol of the rank and file of the host. He could not allow Peter to monopolize the military glory of the crusade. Followed by six hundred knights of whom seventy bore banners the three barons set out for Gaza. The worst fears of Thibaut and Peter were soon fully realized. The count of Bar was slain, Amaury of Montfort was captured, and only a tiny remnant of their followers under the duke of Burgundy escaped to join the host at Ascalon.[11] The loss was so severe that the whole crusading army was completely discouraged. The leaders promptly abandoned their very modest plan of campaign and hastily led their men back to Acre. Peter's own courage and skill had won him renown, but his defiance of discipline was largely responsible for the ignominious failure of the crusade. Still it would be unfair to blame him very severely. Discipline had no place in the traditional ideals of feudal chivalry, and Peter had acted as most of his contemporaries would have in the same circumstances.

Although Peter and his companions remained in the Holy Land for nearly a year after the débâcle before Gaza, their military activities were at an end. Most of the time the army lay in peaceful idleness in Acre. One wild goose chase into the county of Tripoli and several moves to find forage for their horses consumed the energies of the crusaders.[12] The leaders did, however, attempt to gain by negotiation what they had failed to secure by force. The Turkish sultan who ruled in Damascus was at odds with the master of Egypt who controlled southern Palestine. Thibaut and Peter entered into negotiations with the lord of Damascus, and eventually a treaty was concluded. The sultan was to restore all the Christian fiefs and castles to the west of the river Jordan in return for the support of the crusaders against his Egyptian rival. The barons

[11] *Rothelin Eracles*, pp. 538-540 and letter mentioned above.
[12] *Le livre d'Eracles, Recueil des historiens des croisades, Historiens Occidentaux*, II, 415-416. This will be referred to as *Eracles*.

swore to make no peace nor truce with the sultan of Egypt without their ally's consent.[13]   The principal difficulty with this arrangement was that the sultan of Damascus was in a very weak position and seemed unlikely to be able to hold his own for very long.   Then too it was the sultan of Egypt who held the knights who had been captured at Gaza, and the treaty with Damascus seemed to doom them to indefinite imprisonment.   Hence before very long Thibaut and Peter cheerfully forgot their plighted word and began to negotiate with Egypt.[14]

There were a number of reasons for this sudden change in policy.   Undoubtedly the strongest of these was the demand in the army and in fact throughout Christendom that something be done to obtain the release of Amaury of Montfort and his fellow prisoners.   But Peter and Thibaut had a less worthy and more personal motive.   Earl Richard of Cornwall was approaching Acre at the head of a powerful army of English crusaders.   As the French barons were fully aware that they had won no immortal fame as warriors, they were most anxious to prevent Richard from accomplishing anything.   When Thibaut and Peter heard that the earl of Cornwall had landed at Acre, they hastened to come to terms with the sultan of Egypt.   There was to be a ten-year truce during which the Christians were to hold the lands already ceded to them by the agreement with Damascus.   The prisoners taken at Gaza were to be released.   Then without waiting to see the agreement executed, Peter and Thibaut took ship for home.[15]   Richard of Cornwall was left to see to the execution of the treaty and to amuse himself with such inglorious pursuits as completing the fortifications of Ascalon.   Not even the masterly hand of Matthew Paris was able to throw any great aura of glory about Earl Richard's crusade.

Peter and Thibaut probably felt fairly well pleased with themselves as they sailed homeward.   They had accomplished nothing by force of arms, but few crusades did.   Their treaties had considerably extended the boundaries of the kingdom of

[13] *Ibid.*, p. 418.   Matthew Paris, *Chronica maiora*, IV, 64-65.

[14] *Eracles*, p. 419.

[15] *Ibid. Rothelin Eracles*, p. 554.   Letter of Richard of Cornwall in Matthew Paris, *Chronica maiora*, IV, 138-144.

Jerusalem, and the ten-year truce would effectually prevent Earl Richard from winning fame through successful military exploits. Then in all probability these two gay barons had enjoyed their long days at Acre. Certainly the poor knights in the host believed that life there was far too pleasant for the great lords.[16] Peter had even found a good berth for his friend Ralph de Nesle. Before the crusaders set out for home he was married to Alix of Cyprus and was in her right enjoying the highly lucrative post of custodian of the kingdom of Jerusalem for young Conrad of Hohenstaufen.[17] There was only one grave flaw in Peter's satisfaction with his expedition—his brother Count John of Macon had died of disease and his brother-in-law Count Henry of Bar-le-duc had been slain at Gaza. As both John and Henry had always loyally supported Peter in his various enterprises, one may presume that he mourned their loss. For the rest Peter's first crusade to the Holy Land must have been a thoroughly enjoyable affair.

Slippery Elder Statesman

When Peter arrived in France early in 1241, he found the prospects for a peaceful and quiet life anything but promising. His nephews, the sons of Count Henry of Bar-le-duc, were engaged in a fierce controversy over the division of their patrimony. Having been asked to arbitrate the dispute, Peter summoned the contestants to his castle of Fère-en-Tardenois and there divided his late brother-in-law's estate among the quarrelling heirs.[18] Then he turned his steps toward his lands in Poitou where more troubles awaited him. The church of Nantes still hoped to collect damages for the injuries which Peter had inflicted on it when he was duke of Brittany. The clergy had been obliged to let their case rest in suspense while Peter was absent on his crusade, but on his return they were determined to press it vigorously. Still Peter must have been too well accustomed to suits in the ecclesiastical courts to allow

---

[16] *Chansons de croisade,* no. 21.

[17] *Annales de Terre Sainte, Archives de l' Orient Latin,* II, 440. La Monte, *Latin kingdom of Jerusalem,* p. 71.

[18] *Layettes,* III, no. 3846.

this one to worry him much. Far more disturbing were prospective changes in the political organization of Poitou. King Louis' younger brother Alphonse was approaching his majority, and his appanage was to be the county of Poitou. Instead of a distant master ruling through seneschals the barons of Poitou were to have as their lord a royal prince resident in their midst. For the first time since the days of Count Richard Plantagenet the turbulent feudality of the region was to be subject to a strong government. Hugh of Lusignan saw himself faced with the loss of the independence for which he had struggled all his life. Peter's worries were even more acute. If his wife were to die, he would have no rightful claim to her lands. By feudal custom the property which she held as dowry from her first husband would revert to the viscount of Thouars and her own estates would pass to her kinsman and heir, the lord of Commequiers. Thus Peter would lose the most considerable part of his possessions. Now there is no doubt that Peter had every intention of retaining these lands by force if he should survive his wife. His chances of success in such frank usurpation would depend almost entirely on the attitude of the new count of Poitou.

On June 24, 1241, King Louis knighted his brother Alphonse and gave him formal possession of his appanage.[19] The festivities included a magnificent feast held in the great hall of the castle of Saumur. At the royal table sat Alphonse, Peter's nephew Count John of Dreux, Hugh of Lusignan, and Peter himself. King Thibaut of Navarre sat at a separate table. Before him carved the young hereditary seneschal of Champagne, John, lord of Joinville, whose eager eyes drank in the courtly scene which was to find a place in his famous *Histoire de St. Louis*. King Louis was attended by men of higher rank. His brother Robert of Artois served while Count John of Soissons carved the royal meat. Near the king's table stood a guard of honor of thirty knights and many serjeants headed by Humbert of Beaujeu and the lords of Coucy and Bourbon. Another table held Queen Blanche and her ladies while still a fourth gave seats to twenty bishops.[20] It was a noble scene of

---

[19] Matthew Paris, *Chronica maiora*, IV, 138.
[20] Joinville, pp. 34-36.

feudal splendor, and Peter had his due place in it—below the
actual counts but above all other laymen.   Moreover he was
keeping his hand close to the pulse of Poitevin politics.

Peter soon found that he had been wise to seek the benevolence of the new count of Poitou.   As soon as Guy, viscount
of Thouars, had done homage to Alphonse, he addressed to
him a formal demand for the redress of a long list of grievances.   After requesting the restoration of the seneschalship
of Poitou which his father had held in fee and possession of
his wife's patrimony, the barony of Talmont, the viscount
presented his complaints against the former duke of Brittany.
Peter had refused to do homage and perform feudal service
for the baronies of La Garnache and Montaigu which were
fiefs held of the viscounty of Thouars.   In fact he had had
the impudence to announce that his refusal was the result of
the aid which the viscount had given King Louis when Peter
was in revolt against the crown.   Then the viscount complained
that Peter and Margaret had retained the castle of Mareuil-sur-
Lay which was a demesne of the house of Thouars.   How could
Guy perform the services which he owed to Alphonse if his
most powerful vassal refused to fulfill his obligations to him
and usurped the viscount's demesne estates?   He begged the
count of Poitou to force Peter to mend his ways.[21]   There is
no reason for believing that this piteous plea had any effect
whatever.   Not only had Peter himself succeeded in winning
the favor of Alphonse, but the new count of Poitou could ill
afford to offend his mighty neighbor to the north, John, duke of
Brittany.   Alphonse well knew that the barons of Poitou resented his suzerainty and would soon be intriguing with England.   When the time came for open war, Peter and his son
would be invaluable allies.

By the end of 1241 the situation in Poitou was drawing
rapidly toward a crisis.   Urged on by his imperious wife, the
count of La Marche raised the standard of revolt.   About him
rallied the Poitevin barons who had for years been accustomed
to follow the leadership of the house of Lusignan.   Henry III
and even Alphonse's father-in-law, Raymond of Toulouse,

---

[21] *Layettes*, III, no. 3628.

promised the rebels their support. Count Hugh also approached the barons who had been his associates in the earlier leagues against the crown. Thibaut of Navarre and Hugh of Burgundy lent willing ears to his schemes, but Peter refused to become involved. One chronicler asserts that he went so far as to inform King Louis of the baronial plot.[22] Meanwhile the king had decided that the time had come to subdue Poitou thoroughly. Too often had the Capetian monarchs bought the Lusignans only to have them resell themselves to the English a few months later. Hence Louis summoned his host to muster at Chinon toward the end of April 1242 for an expedition against the Poitevin rebels and their allies. The king of Navarre and the duke of Burgundy failed to appear, but Peter was on hand to play his part in the campaign against his former ally.[23] For the first time since 1226 he was to march behind rather than against the royal standard of King Louis.

Peter's adherence was of great strategic value to the royal cause because it made inevitable the prompt submission of the house of Thouars. The viscount and his relatives ruled the most important strongholds of northern Poitou and their inclinations were decidely pro-English. If they supported the Lusignan masters of central and southern Poitou, Louis could not hope to make much progress before Henry III arrived with his English troops. But the barons of the Thouars family could not contemplate with equanimity the prospect of simultaneous attacks on their lands by the royal army and the formidable lord of Montaigu. Late in April the viscount, his brother, and his nephew hastened to Chinon, did homage to count Alphonse, and surrendered their castles for the duration of the war.[24] Their submission cleared King Louis' path to the northernmost line of Lusignan strongholds. On May 9 Montreuil-Bonnin opened its gates to the royal host, and by July 20 Louis had captured all the hostile castles north of the river Charente except the great fortress of Lusignan. Meanwhile Henry III

[22] Mousket, II, 677. A. Thomas, "Une chanson française sur la bataille de Taillebourg," *Annales du Midi*, IV (1892), 365, 368.
[23] *Ibid*. Charles Bémont, "La campagne de Poitou, 1242-1243," *Annales du Midi*, V (1893), 293.
[24] *Layettes*, II, no. 2972.

had arrived in Poitou and was watching the crossings over the Charente. On July 21 King Louis routed the English army at Taillebourg and a few days later he occupied Saintes.[25] Hugh of Lusignan was completely discouraged. He had seen his proud castles fall with astounding rapidity and his stepson driven ignominiously out of Poitou. He sent a messenger to Peter, "one traitor to another," as Matthew Paris kindly remarked, to ask him to intercede for him with King Louis. Peter and the bishop of Saintes had an interview with the king and learned the terms on which Louis would accept the submission of Count Hugh. These terms were extremely severe. All the castles, demesnes, and fees which had been occupied by the royal army during the war were to remain in the possession of Count Alphonse. Matthew Paris, who had a profound dislike for Peter, accused him of being an unfaithful emissary. According to his story Peter publicly begged Louis to be merciful to Hugh, but privately urged the king to be as severe as possible.[26] While Matthew's animus against Peter and his love for scandal-mongering make his testimony unreliable, his account may be true. As Peter's wife had died in the previous autumn, he was peculiarly anxious to secure the good will of Louis and Alphonse.[27] If he believed that his Poitevin fiefs were at stake, a little disloyalty toward Hugh would not have troubled Peter's conscience unduly. Still Louis was convinced of the necessity for breaking the power of the Lusignans, and he probably required no urging to deal harshly with the defeated head of that house. Hugh of Lusignan accepted the king's terms and made his submission. Then he and Peter led a royal army against Hugh's recent ally, Count Raymond of Toulouse.[28] Peter's loyalty and good service to Louis and Alphonse received their anticipated reward. For the rest of his life he held the lands of Margaret of Montaigu in defiance of the rights of the viscount of Thouars and the lord of Com-

---

[25] Bémont, *La campagne de Poitou*, pp. 294-307.

[26] Matthew Paris, *Chronica maiora*, IV, 214-216. Matthew considered that Peter had betrayed Henry III in 1234 and had behaved very badly toward Richard of Cornwall in Palestine.

[27] Morice, *Preuves*, I, 921.

[28] *Layettes*, II, no. 2980. Matthew Paris, *Chronica maiora*, IV, 216.

mequiers.   He also remained on excellent terms with his son-in-law, the younger Hugh of Lusignan.[29]   Clearly Peter had not lost his ability to keep friends in all possible camps.

Soon after the restoration of peace in Poitou Peter found himself faced with a renewal of his old controversy with the church of Nantes.   In 1240 his bitter enemy, Bishop Robert, had been elevated to the patriarchate of Jerusalem.   Robert's successor, Galeran, came into office determined to force Peter and John to make restitution for the injuries which they had inflicted on the see of Nantes.   As soon as Peter returned from his crusade, the bishop secured the appointment of a papal commission headed by the archbishop of Bourges.   On August 16, 1241, two Breton abbots were ordered to summon Peter to appear at Bourges on September 19.[30]   But fortune smiled on the lord of Montaigu.   On August 22, 1241, Pope Gregory IX died, and Peter could easily ignore the summons to Bourges. Even more helpful was the fact that the papal throne stood vacant, except for the one month's reign of Celestine IV, until June 1243.   In March 1244 the new pope, Innocent IV, ordered the bishop of Angers to investigate the grievances of the bishop of Nantes.   Peter and John were summoned to appear before the pope's delegate in the cathedral of Nantes on June 9.[31]   In all probability Peter followed his usual custom of ignoring such citations.   At any rate the controversy went merrily on.

Peter had always been inclined to answer the attacks of the church with spirited counter-offensives, and he was now in a most favorable position for carrying out such a maneuver.   In his previous conflicts with the clergy he had been continually hampered by political considerations, but now he was essentially retired from feudal politics.   Moreover in October 1245 he took the cross in company with King Louis and a large part of the chivalry of France and thus was clothed once more in the protecting mantle of a crusader.[32]   Soon Peter's fertile brain evolved a brilliant scheme for baiting his lifelong foes.   In

[29] Morice, Preuves, I, 930. Layettes, II, no. 3569.

[30] Morice, Preuves, I, 921.

[31] Ibid., columns 923-924.

[32] Nangis, Gesta, Historiens de France, XX, 352. Matthew Paris, Chronica maiora, IV, 490.

November 1246 a group of barons issued a remarkable manifesto. They had banded themselves together to defend their rights against the usurpations of the clergy. The activities of the league were to be directed by an executive committee consisting of the duke of Burgundy, Peter, and the counts of Angoulême and St. Pol. The members of the association swore to take such common action as this committee should suggest. Each member would contribute one per cent of his annual revenue to a common fund which would be used by the committee to further the ends of the association.[33] Unfortunately we do not know the names of the nineteen men who affixed their seals to this declaration, but the composition of the executive committee shows that Peter was the dominant figure. The duke of Burgundy had married his niece and had always been his close ally. The count of Angoulême was his son-in-law, the younger Hugh of Lusignan, who had inherited the county of Angoulême at his mother's death. The count of St. Pol was Peter's kinsman and long-time associate, Hugh of Châtillon. In short Peter sought allies and a war chest for his current struggle with the church. As a matter of fact the league probably disappointed its founder. The manifesto was prepared to receive some four times as many seals as were actually attached to it. Still if Peter's purpose was to alarm and annoy the pope, he was eminently successful. A blast of papal missives demanded the denunciation and excommunication of all men in any way connected with this league against the church.[34] Nothing is known of the history of this child of Peter's ingenious brain. In all probability it fell to pieces before the papal fury, but Peter may well have gained the pope's agreement to a favorable compromise in the controversy with the bishop of Nantes as the price for abandoning his anti-clerical league.

During the summer of 1248 the long-standing quarrel between the dukes of Brittany and the church of Nantes was settled for the time being. Innocent IV decreed that Peter was to pay certain damages, but many other items in the bishop's

[33] *Ibid.*, pp. 591-592. *Layettes*, II, no. 3569.

[34] *Registres d'Innocent IV* (ed. Élie Berger, *Bibliothèque des écoles françaises d'Athènes et de Rome*, second series), nos. 2951-2952.

list of grievances were disallowed.[35] As the bishop won most of the political questions at issue, the papal decision must have been a severe blow to John of Brittany, but Peter came off very easily. Moreover it is most unlikely that he ever paid any of the damages assessed against him. When the final decision was rendered, Peter was preparing to follow King Louis to the Holy Land, and no one expected a prospective crusader to pay money to anyone. Certainly the church could not gracefully demand payment from resources which were pledged to the sacred cause.

Last Adventure

Little more is known about Peter's activities during the years between his two crusades. While the castle of La Garnache remained his official seat, he appears to have spent most of his time on his estates near Paris. Once his wife had died and Poitou had been reduced to order by the firm hand of Count Alphonse, there was no longer any need for Peter to reside in his baronies of Montaigu and La Garnache. He was a Frenchman in the narrow contemporary sense of the word, a native of the Ile-de-France and a scion of the Capetian lords of Paris. He had passed his best years as an exile in Brittany and La Vendée, but now in his old age he could return to the pleasant land of his youth. Moreover Peter's love of power and prestige drew him toward the royal court and the seats of his relatives. In Poitou he was a mere rear-vassal of Count Alphonse, but in France he was the king's kinsman and the senior member of the great house of Dreux. Now that Peter was politically innocuous King Louis could and did accord due honor to this senior prince of the Capetian blood who had known and served his father and grandfather. Throughout the pages of Joinville's memoirs Peter appears as a man of high influence whose counsel competed in the royal ear with that of the king's own brothers. His status during this period is most clearly shown by the titles which were used to designate him. In his own charters he modestly called himself Peter of Braine, knight, but his contemporaries were unwilling to apply to him so

[35] Morice, *Preuves*, I, 935-939.

humble an appellation. The royal and papal chanceries addressed him as Peter, former count of Brittany, and in ordinary usage he was simply Count Peter of Brittany.[36] Although he was actually a minor baron, Peter was considered a count or at least a count emeritus.

According to mediæval convention the principal concern of a man who was approaching his sixtieth year should be to secure a sure passage into heaven. Peter had never been one to do things by halves. Whereas Thibaut of Champagne was convinced that one crusade to the Orient would assure him of eternal bliss, Peter made two such expeditions during the last ten years of his life. While it is true that his formation of the league against the clergy was a slight deviation from his path to salvation, when he undertook that enterprise he was already vowed to the crusade and assured of the plenary indulgence which was the reward of the crusader. Only sudden death before the crusade started could seriously endanger Peter's soul. But before he departed on his second eastern adventure, he took a precaution that no wise Christian could neglect—he made his testament. Although the document itself has been lost, the names of Peter's executors and some of his bequests are known from other sources. The men whom he chose to carry out his last wishes give a clear indication of the concentration of Peter's interests in the Paris region during his last years. Instead of the Breton ecclesiastics who had been his confidants in former years, he selected Reginald, bishop of Paris, and Walter, prior of St. Giles-under-Chilly.[37] The priory of St. Giles was a daughter house of the Parisian monastery of St. Catherine of the Vale of Scholars which had been founded by Philip Augustus in gratitude for the victory of Bouvines. The priory had been established in the valley between Peter's villages of Chilly and Longjumeau by his brother Count John of Macon. Shortly before Peter departed on his last crusade he gave it £40 a year to be paid from the revenues of Chilly.[38]

[36] *Ibid.*, columns 921, 930. Levron, *Catalogue*, no. 271. *Historiens de France*, XXIII, 727. *Layettes*, II, no. 3569; III, no. 3628. Mousket, II, 667. Joinville, pp. 34, 84.

[37] *Gallia Christiana*, VII, *Instrumenta*, p. 280.

[38] *Ibid.*, pp. 863-865.

Prior Walter was clearly in high favor with Peter and was probably the active executor. The function of the bishop of Paris was to support Peter's last wishes with the full authority of the church. Unfortunately only four of Peter's bequests are known. The monastery of St. Catherine, the mother house of Walter's priory of St. Giles, received £1,000 of Paris and another establishment a similar sum in the money of Tours. The cathedral church of Paris was given a bequest sufficient to produce a revenue of £100 of Paris a year to purchase masses for the donor's soul on each anniversary of his death. The abbey of St. Victor received £50 of Tours.[39] Thus Peter made sure that these churches would resound annually with masses for the welfare of his soul. All these establishments were in the neighborhood of Paris, but it is by no means certain that Peter made no other bequests. The publication of the *Obitu-aires* for the province of Tours might well reveal additional benefactions. One can merely say that Peter's executors were prelates of the Ile-de-France and his known bequests were to houses in that region. Incidentally the size of the gifts shows that Peter was far from poverty-stricken. When one considers that during the coming crusade he was to loan King Louis £8,000, it is possible to form a vague idea of the size of Peter's fortune.

Our knowledge of Peter's part in the crusade of 1248-1251 is confined to a few episodes. An elderly baron of no feudal importance was bound to be in a subordinate position in an army which was led by King Louis and his brothers, and mediæval chroniclers had little interest in subordinates. Fortunately young John of Joinville liked and admired the former duke of Brittany, and here and there in his charming, rambling, and garrulous memoirs one catches a brief glimpse of Peter. His blood, age, and prestige as a soldier gave him a place in the councils of the crusading chieftains, but he could not exert much influence on the arrogant and reckless royal princes. In battle Peter was simply one minor captain among many who followed where Louis and his brothers led.

[39] *Obituaires de la province de Sens, Recueil des historiens de la France, Obituaires*, I, 142, 566, 651, 687.

On August 28, 1258, the crusading fleet sailed from Aigues-mortes, and on September 17 it arrived at the island of Cyprus where the crusaders were to spend the winter.[40] While they were resting on that peaceful isle, the leaders decided to make an expedition against Cairo, the capital of the Turkish sultan who ruled over Palestine. But as mediæval armies were never in a hurry and the fleet was at the mercy of capricious winds, it was the end of May before the crusaders left Cyprus for the Egyptian coast. There an astounding success awaited them— the great city of Damietta, caught unprepared, fell without serious resistance. King Louis was delighted, but he was rather at a loss as to how to use his victory. The delta of the Nile was absolutely impassable in summer when the waters were high, and Count Alphonse of Poitou had not yet joined the host. Hence the army sat idly in Damietta from early June to late November while the enemy prepared to resist its march toward Cairo.

When Count Alphonse finally arrived, King Louis held a council of war. Peter and many of his fellow barons were opposed to a march against Cairo from Damietta.[41] A glance at a map will show that they had good grounds for this opinion. Damietta was in the center of the coast of the Nile's delta, and a march to Cairo would involve crossing at least three major and many minor branches of the great river. Each of these streams would form an almost impregnable line of defense for the Turks. To an experienced and careful soldier like Peter the project must have seemed utterly insane. He advised the king to sail along the coast and lay siege to Alexandria. As that city was on the extreme western edge of the delta, a march from it to Cairo would not be hampered by the branches of the Nile. As a matter of fact, however, Peter probably had no enthusiasm for going to Cairo by any route. Alexandria was certain to offer a stubborn resistance, and the crusaders could spend the rest of the season in a pleasant siege within reach of their ships. Why march into the interior of Egypt to fight the

[40] Reinhold Röhricht, "Der Kreuzzug Louis IX gegen Damiette," *Kleine Studien zur Geschichte der Kreuzzuge* (Berlin, 1890), p. 15.

[41] Joinville, p. 64.

infidel when he could be found on the coast? Peter was no fanatic who burned to rescue the Holy Land. He sought adventure and his soul's salvation, but he preferred to find them as comfortably and safely as possible.

Peter's counsel passed unheeded. King Louis accepted the advice of his reckless young brother, Count Robert of Artois, and started the army on its almost hopeless march toward Cairo. This is no place to retell the well-known and tragic story of King Louis' Egyptian campaign. At the battle of Mansourah Peter was attached to the first division which was commanded by the count of Artois. In complete defiance of his brother's express orders and all the requirements of sound strategy Count Robert refused to wait for the other divisions and led his troops headlong into the town of Mansourah where they were overwhelmed by the immensely superior numbers of the enemy. Robert of Artois, the master of the Templars, and Ralph of Coucy were killed, but Peter and the count of Soissons managed to cut their way out. Joinville furnishes a delightful glimpse of Peter as he retreated from Mansourah.

> Straight toward us who guarded the little bridge came Count Peter of Brittany who came from the direction of Mansourah, and he was wounded with a sword cut across his face so that the blood fell into his mouth. He sat a handsome and well-equipped war horse. His reins had been dropped onto the pommel of his saddle, and he clasped the pommel with both hands in order that his men who were behind him and who pressed him greatly might not unseat him. He certainly seemed to value them little, for as he spat the blood from his mouth he said very often "Look! By the head of God, have you seen such a rabble?" [42]

Peter passed on presumably to join the division commanded by King Louis. His prowess had enabled him to escape the Turkish swords, but his respite from death was to be a short one. Soon after the battle of Mansourah he fell prisoner to the Turks with King Louis and most of the crusading barons.[43] Weakened by wounds and advanced years, Peter found the hardships of imprisonment too much for him. When the captives were finally released, he was desperately sick. The counts

[42] *Ibid.*, p. 84.
[43] *Ibid.*, p. 118. *Rothelin Eracles*, p. 615.

of Flanders and Soissons placed him on a ship and set sail for home, but Peter died before they reached France.[44]   Perhaps this was the chief triumph of his career.   Death on a crusade was a sure guarantee of salvation.   Peter had spent a large part of his life under excommunication and yet succeeded in dying in the odor of sanctity.   The " Scourge of the Clergy " would pass serenely into heaven.

[44] Joinville, p. 134.

APPENDIX 1

THE SIEGE OF BELLÊME

M. Berger places the siege of Bellême in January 1229.[1] While this date is consistent with the meagre indications given by William of Nangis, Berger expressly disavows any confidence in that chronicler's chronology.[2] He does, however, accept Nangis' statement that the siege took place in mid-winter. M. Berger then points out that from what is known about King Louis' itinerary the siege could have been conducted by him either in January 1229 or January 1230. So far I fully concur in Berger's conclusions—but I consider January 1230 the more acceptable date.

In presenting his arguments for January 1229 M. Berger relies on two contemporary documents. One of these is the letter of defiance, dated January 20, 1230, which Peter sent to the king. The extreme importance of this document and its unavailability in print seem to justify giving it in full.[3]

' Universis praesentes litteras inspecturis. P. Dux Brittanniae Comes Richmond Sal. Noveritis quod nos mittimus regi Franciae per T. templarium latorem praesentium has praesentes litteras. Rex adjornaverat comitem Britanniae ad dominicam post natale apud Meledunum, cui diei ipse dominus rex noluit interesse. Comes illuc misit, et regi mandavit, quod terminus quem ei posuerat, non erat competens, quia non erat de quadraginta diebus, et propter hoc requisivit alium terminum competentem ab illis qui erant loco regis ibidem ad

[1] Berger devotes a long footnote to his arguments for this date. *Blanche de Castille*, p. 125, note 2. Unless otherwise noted references to Berger are to this note.

[2] It is, however, interesting to notice that while Nangis places the siege of Bellême late in 1228 which could be January 1229, he makes it follow the invasion of Champagne which actually took place in the summer of 1229. Hence his order of events indicates January 1230 as the date of the siege. *Chronicon*, I, 177-179. *Gesta, Historiens de France*, XX, 314-316.

[3] It is printed in Du Cange's edition of Joinville of 1688. Berger, *Blanche de Castille*, p. 125, note 1. I have used it in Thomas Johnes' translation of Du Cange into English. Johnes gives the document in Latin. *Memoirs of John, lord de Joinville* (translated by Thomas Johnes, 1807), I, 273-274.

faciendum quod debent, et propter hoc comes fecit scribi omnes
queremonias suas et iniurias, quas rex et mater sua et sui ei fecerant,
et scriptum illud super queremoniis traditum fuit illis qui erant loco
regis.   Quod scriptum sicut factum fuit intelligi comiti, noluit regina
quod ostenderetur baronibus et probis hominibus Franciae, imo aliter
eis fecit intelligi voluntatem suam; comes nunquam potuit habere
emendationem de iniuriis, et malis sibi factis per regem et suos.   Nisi
hoc quod ipse rex fecit desaisiri eundem comitem de eo quod ab ipso
tenebat in Andegavia, unde erat homo suus, et castrum suum de
Belismo, quod similiter ab ipso tenebat, obsedit, et terram suam fecit
destrui, et homines suos fecit interfici.

' Haec mala cum aliis malis fecit ei rex sine defectu iuris quem comes
fecisset, et sine eo quod numquam fuisset adjornatus per regem, nec
ante, nec post, nisi ad dictum diem propter has iniurias, et propter
alias de quibus comes non potuit habere emendationem, mandat ipse
comes regi quod se non tenet plus pro homine suo, imo ab homagio suo
recedit, et in hoc recessu intelligit comes diffidationem.   Actum anno
gratiae, 1229, die Dominica in Octavis B. Hilarii.'

Berger draws two important inferences from this letter—that
it was written after the fall of Bellême and more than a month
after the meeting at Melun. But the document does not seem to
furnish adequate grounds for either of these conclusions.   The
letter says nothing about the capture of Bellême. Duke Peter
complains that the king has seized his Angevin fiefs and besieged his castle of Bellême.   Had this stronghold already been
taken, some such word as *cepit* rather than *obsedit* would be
expected.   While the use of *obsedit* does not prove that the
siege was still in progress on January 20, 1230, it suggests that
conclusion.   It certainly cannot be taken as evidence that the
castle had already been captured.   M. Berger's second point
appears even more difficult to maintain.   Obviously his theory
that the siege took place in January 1229 forces him to date
the meeting at Melun in December 1228.   But Peter writing
in January 1230 says simply " the Sunday after Christmas " with
no reference to any year.   This would naturally lead one to presume that he meant the preceding Sunday after Christmas or
December 30, 1229.   Berger tacitly admits this.   He argues
that the contents of the letter make clear that it was written far
more than a month after the meeting at Melun.   I cannot accept
this conclusion.   Duke Peter's messengers had returned to tell
him what had happened at the meeting.   The royal forces had

seized the duke's Angevin fiefs and laid siege to Bellême. If one assumes that Blanche was shocked and surprised by Peter's failure to obey the king and had to make all military preparations after the event, then the proceedings do seem rather rapid. But it is far more probable that the queen regent was fully prepared for the duke's contumacy. In that case there would have been plenty of time. The fact that Louis was certainly in Anjou early in January 1230 supports this view. In short it seems to me that only overwhelming evidence to the contrary can justify a refusal to accept the clear implication of the letter that the summons to Melun was for December 30, 1229. No such evidence can be found in the document. Thus my conclusions from this letter are the exact opposite of those formed by M. Berger. To me it clearly states that the summons was for December 29, 1229, and strongly suggests that the siege of Bellême was in progress on January 20, 1230.

The second document used by M. Berger is a list of men who were summoned to arms by a rear-ban issued by Count Thibaut of Champagne. The roll bears no date, but its editor, M. Longnon, places it between July 1227 and March 1229.[4] Berger points out that unless the attack on Bellême took place in January 1229, we know of no expedition during this period which might account for the calling-out of the feudal levy of Champagne. As Joinville seems to state that Thibaut joined the expedition against Bellême with three hundred knights, Berger considers his point proved.[5] This conclusion is, however, open to three serious objections. In the first place there is reason to mistrust the terminus *ad quem* established by M. Longnon. A section of the roll bears the heading *de dotalicio Blanche comitisse*. As the Countess-Dowager Blanche died in March 1229, Longnon assumes that the summons was issued before that date. This seems to presume too great an affection for accuracy among Thibaut's clerks. They undoubtedly made out the list of vassals to be summoned from the most recent roll of the fees owing service to their lord. Until a new roll was drawn up, this would contain a division for the countess' dowry. It

---

[4] *Documents relatifs au comté de Champagne et de Brie 1172-1361* (ed. Auguste Longnon, Paris, 1901), I, 175-177.

[5] *Blanche de Castille*, pp. 123-124.

would not be very disturbing to find this heading retained on any such summons prior to 1249 when a new roll was made. In short one might say that the terminus *ad quem* for this document should be placed within a few years after the countess' death, but even this assertion would be hard to prove. The second objection to Berger's argument concerns his use of Joinville. As this historian was born in 1225 and probably wrote this part of his work in 1305, his knowledge of our period is hazy at best, and he speaks with due caution.[6] After describing the baronial agreement that Peter should revolt, and that if the king summoned the host against him, his allies would attend with only two knights each, Joinville says that Thibaut joined Louis with three hundred knights. The support of the count of Champagne enabled Louis to force Peter to make peace and surrender the counties of Anjou and Perche.[7] Joinville does not mention the attack on Bellême. Duke Peter's treaty with the king by which he gave up his Angevin fiefs and Bellême in Perche was made in 1234. The expedition described by Joinville could have been that against Peter and Henry III in 1230, the invasion of Brittany in 1231, or that of 1234. Thibaut certainly played an important part in the campaigns of 1230 and 1231 and he probably did in 1234 also.[8] Thus Joinville cannot be used to prove that Thibaut led three hundred knights to the siege of Bellême. The third objection to M. Berger's conclusion is a little more tenuous. It seems doubtful whether feudal custom would have allowed Count Thibaut to summon his rear-ban for the expedition against Bellême. The rear-ban was the levy *en masse* of all men able to bear arms and was supposed to be used only in case of an invasion of the fief by an enemy.[9]

[6] Auguste Molinier, *Les sources de l'histoire de France* (Paris, 1901-1906), III, 104-107.

[7] Joinville, p. 27.

[8] Jubainville, *Catalogue*, no. 2037. *Layettes*, II, no. 2056. *Paga militum etc., Historiens de France*, XXI, 222.

[9] A. Luchaire, *Manuel des institutions françaises* (Paris, 1892), p. 195. *La summa de legibus Normannie in curia laicali, in Coutumiers de Normandie* (ed. Joseph Tardif, Paris, 1896), II, 69. This passage states clearly that the *retrobannium* could only be issued to defend the duchy from invasion. Still the question is a complicated one, and it is impossible to state categorically that Thibaut could not issue a rear-ban to support the king.

Such an occasion can easily be found in this period. Either of the baronial attacks on Champagne which were launched in 1229 and 1230 would have justified the calling-out of the rear-ban. As the earlier of these took place only a few months after the death of the countess-dowager, the hypothesis that it was the occasion for the summons would do very little violence to M. Longnon's date. Thus it seems to me that there is no clear proof that this document should be placed before March 1229, no evidence whatever that Thibaut was present at the siege of Bellême, and sound reasons for believing that if he did go on that expedition, he did not summon his rear-ban for it. If these conclusions be accepted, this document has no bearing on the date of the siege of Bellême.

The examination of the evidence used by M. Berger has, I believe, shown that his reasons for placing the siege of Bellême in January 1229 are essentially unsound. The fact that Duke Peter in his letter of January 20, 1230, used *obsedit* in speaking of the attack on Bellême and failed to indicate any year when stating that he had been summoned to Melun for the Sunday after Christmas indicates January 1230 as the date of the siege. There is another consideration which tends to support this date. Why did Queen Blanche summon Peter to appear at Melun? Berger states that in accordance with the agreement made at a baronial conference the duke opened hostilities in the autumn of 1228.[10] He gives no reference for this assertion, and it will not bear close inspection. If Peter had already begun the war, there was no need to waste time summoning him to court. An attack on the king's lands would certainly justify counter-measures. The only basis for Berger's statement lies in Joinville's assertion that Peter rose in revolt in accordance with the baronial plan. But Joinville is clearly describing the whole course of Peter's rebellion to 1234. His account ends with the duke making peace with Louis and surrendering his Angevin fiefs and Bellême. Hence the revolt he speaks of could easily apply to the events of 1230. In short there is no clear evidence that Peter committed any act of rebellion in the autumn of 1228, and if he had, it would not explain his summons to Melun.

[10] *Blanche de Castille*, p. 123.

Now William of Nangis and Vincent of Beauvais say nothing about the meeting at Melun, but they both make it perfectly clear that Bellême was attacked because Peter had formed an alliance with Henry III.[11] The treaty of Vendôme bound the duke to make no agreement with England. If he violated his promise and failed to appear in the king's court to justify himself within forty days after being summoned, the lands which he held under the terms of the treaty would be forfeited.[12] Thus if Peter made an alliance with Henry, Blanche could summon him. If he did not obey, she could seize his Angevin fiefs and Bellême. Ordinarily a contumacious vassal was entitled to another forty days warning. Only under the treaty of Vendôme could immediate action be justified. Therefore it seems highly probable that Peter was summoned to Melun to answer the charge that he had made a treaty with England. But there is no evidence that he made any such alliance as early as the autumn of 1228. The English rolls are very complete, and an agreement with Peter would not be likely to be unrecorded. Furthermore, if the duke had allied with Henry III at that time, he would have received his English fiefs before October 1229. It was in fact at this last time that Peter visited England and thus gave Blanche an excuse to proceed against him under the treaty of Vendôme. In the autumn of 1228 the summons to Melun would have been outrageous and Blanche's attack on Bellême completely unjustified. Both would have been reasonable and proper a year later.

Finally there is some evidence that hostilities between Peter and the royal government did in fact commence early in 1230. In the inquest held in 1235 for Alan of Acigné there appears this statement—*comes tenuit terram illam ex quo comes fecit*

---

[11] Vincent de Beauvais, *Memoriale temporum, Monumenta Germaniae historica, Scriptores,* XXIV, 161. Nangis, *Chronicon,* I, 179; *Gesta, Historiens de France,* XX, 316. Levron states that Blanche attacked Bellême because Peter had been repairing its fortifications in defiance of the treaty of Vendôme. *Pierre Mauclerc,* p. 85. There can be litte doubt that Peter repaired Bellême, but as he had obtained its custody in 1226, 1228 seems rather late to begin. Nangis places the strengthening of Bellême in 1226-1227. *Gesta, Historiens de France,* XX, 312. None of the chroniclers gives Peter's repairs as the reason for Blanche's attack on the fortress.

[12] *Layettes,* II, no. 1922.

priman chivaucheam apud Abrincas super Dominum Regem.[13] The exact meaning of this passage is not quite clear. While it may mean that there were several raids made by Peter into the Avranches region and this happened at the time of the first one, it seems more reasonable to interpret it as saying that Peter's first *chevauché* against the king was an invasion of that district. Now the beginning of Peter's warlike activities in southwestern Normandy can be dated with fair certainty. In February 1230 the duke issued letters ordering his officers to protect the abbey of Mont-Saint-Michel *toto tempore guerre nostre*.[14] As the possessions of the abbey lay between the Breton border and Avranches, it seems safe to assume that these letters of protection were issued just before the *chivau-cheam apud Abrincas* mentioned in the inquest. If this reasoning is sound, Peter's first act of hostility against Louis was a raid into Normandy in February 1230.

In conclusion I am forced to admit that there is no evidence by which the siege of Bellême can be dated with absolute certainty. But in order to place it in January 1229 one must distort the import of the chief document, Peter's letter of defiance. Furthermore Blanche's procedure as set forth in that letter and the chronicle of Reims appears justified and reasonable only if one assumes that it followed Peter's visit to England in October 1229.[15] Finally the passage quoted from the inquest of 1235 indicates that the war started early in 1230. For these reasons I have placed the siege of Bellême in January 1230 and have developed my chronology on that basis.

---

[13] *Testes domini Alani de Assegni contra comitem super dampnis suis in terra uxoris sue.* Archives nationales, Trésor des chartes, J. 626, no. 148.

[14] Levron, *Catalogue*, no. 128 and pp. 263-264.

[15] *Ménestrel de Reims*, p. 186.

APPENDIX II

MARGARET OF MONTAIGU

While I am unable to offer a conclusive solution of the problems connected with the genealogy of Margaret of Montaigu and her right to the baronies of Montaigu and La Garnache, it seems worth while to review the available evidence in the hope of clearing away established errors and laying a firm foundation for future research. M. René Blanchard made Margaret the sister of a Maurice, lord of Montaigu, who issued a number of charters between 1195 and 1203.[1] He based this conclusion on the fact that in 1203 Margaret and her husband, Hugh of Thouars, appeared as lord and lady of Montaigu even though two sons of Maurice survived as lords of the lesser barony of Commequiers.[2] Now the custom of the major fief of Bas-Poitou, the viscounty of Thouars, provided for the succession of younger brothers ahead of the sons of the eldest, but there is no evidence that this rule ever applied to sisters. Still Blanchard considered this the only possible explanation of how Margaret became *heres legitima de Montis Acuti*.[3] As a matter of fact this theory rests on a misinterpretation of the evidence. In 1202 this Maurice, lord of Montaigu, issued a charter in which he gave a fairly complete genealogy of his family. His grandfather named Urvoidus had had three sons—Brient, Herbert, and Hugh. Brient was the father of Maurice who himself had two surviving sons, Maurice and Brient.[4] Blanchard assumed that this was the genealogy of the barons of Montaigu. But charters of 1093 and 1099 contain the name of Urvoidus of Commequiers.[5] Then a charter of about 1130 mentions

[1] " Cartulaire de Rays," *Archives historiques du Poitou*, XXVIII (1898), cxxvi-cxxvii.

[2] Morice, *Preuves*, I, 797. *Cartulaires du Bas-Poitou* (ed. Paul Marchegay, Les Roches-Baritaud, 1877), pp. 147, 191-192, 223-224.

[3] M. de la Boutetière, " Dons d'hommes au xiii° siècle en Bas-Poitou," *Archives historiques du Poitou*, I (1872), 81-82.

[4] *Cartulaires du Bas-Poitou*, pp. 145-146.

[5] *Ibid.*, pp. 17, 22-23, 344-345.

Brient of Commequiers and his brothers Herbert and Hugh.[6] When one considers that after the death of Maurice, lord of Montaigu, his two sons were successively lords of Commequiers, it becomes clear that this genealogy was that of the lords of the latter barony. Then the document of 1099 mentioned above proves that Urvoidus at least was not lord of Montaigu. In that year the barons of the viscounty of Thouars agreed to give an annual revenue to a religious house, and their names were listed in the charter. At the head of this list appears Maurice of Montaigu who promised twenty shillings a year—more than any other baron. Far down the roll of names comes Urvoidus of Commequiers with a pledge of five shillings.[7] Thus of the men mentioned in the charter of 1202 only Maurice himself is known to have held the title of lord of Montaigu. His grandfather, father, and sons appeared only as lords of Commequiers. After the deaths of Margaret and her second husband Peter of Dreux, Maurice's grandson, Maurice, lord of Commequiers and Belleville, became lord of Montaigu as well.[8]

The extremely scanty evidence will go no farther, but it seems possible to draw some very tentative conclusions. Either Brient I or Maurice I of Commequiers married into the house of the barons of Montaigu. The introduction of the name Maurice into the family of Commequiers suggests that it was Brient who made this alliance. I would like to advance the hypothesis that the male line of the lords of Montaigu, descendants of the Maurice of Montaigu of 1099, became extinct, and the inheritance fell to Margaret of Montaigu. Margaret's heir apparent was her kinsman Maurice, lord of Commequiers. I strongly suspect that when Maurice bore the title lord of Montaigu he did so as custodian for Margaret who had not yet married. The reader will find at the end of this appendix a genealogical chart of the houses of Commequiers and Montaigu with my guesses in italics.

There is no evidence whatever that I can find to explain Margaret's right to inherit the barony of La Garnache. It is clear,

<hr />

[6] M. de la Boutetière, "Cartulaire de Coudrie," *Archives historiques du Poitou*, II (1873), 153-154.

[7] *Cartulaires du Bas-Poitou*, pp. 22-23, 344-345.

[8] *Ibid.*, pp. 171-173.

however, that she derived her claim from her position as heiress of the house of Montaigu because both baronies passed to Maurice of Belleville after the death of Peter of Dreux.[9]   It seems safe to assume that some previous lord of Montaigu had married into the house of La Garnache.   When the male line of the latter barony became extinct at the death of Peter V, the fief passed to the heiress of Montaigu.

[9] *Ibid.*

THE HOUSES OF MONTAIGU AND COMMEQUIERS

(The words italicized in parenthesis and the broken lines indicate guesses)

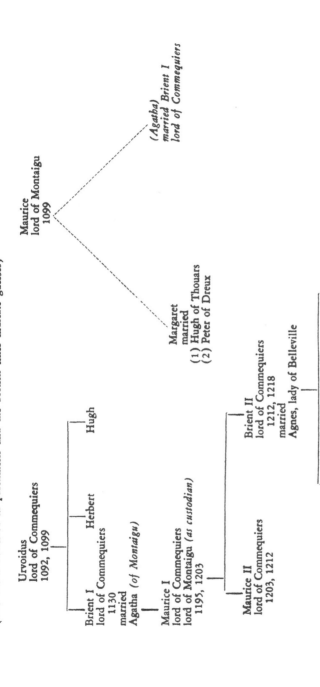

APPENDIX III

OLIVER OF MACHECOUL

Peter's son Oliver, generally known as Oliver of Machecoul, has been the subject of much speculation most of which has been based on inadequate knowledge of the available evidence. In general scholars have accepted him as the son of Peter by his second wife, Margaret of Montaigu.[1] M. Blanchard, however, has very ably opposed this view. He quotes an epitaph which states "Cy gist dame Nicolle, la mère monsour Oliver de Mackecou" and points out that the only other Oliver of Machecoul was Oliver II who was certainly the son of Eustachie of Vitré.[2] This then is a positive statement that Oliver's mother was named Nicole. Only overwhelming evidence that Margaret was his mother could outweigh it.

As a matter of fact even without this epitaph there is ample reason for refusing to accept Oliver as Margaret's son. Margaret was married to Hugh of Thouars as early as 1203.[3] Taking twelve years old as a safe minimum age for marriage, she must have been at least thirty-nine when Peter married her in 1230. When one considers that she had lived with Hugh of Thouars for twenty-seven years without having any children, it appears unlikely that she should have born Peter a son.[4] Only the delight of nature in freakish pranks, especially in the realm of procreation, might cause one to decline to accept this argument as conclusive. Fortunately there is an even stronger proof that Oliver was not Margaret's son—he inherited none of her lands. It is most difficult to conceive how Margaret could have been the *heres legitima* of Montaigu and yet transmit

---

[1] Bertrand de Broussillon, *La maison de Craon* (Paris, 1893), I, 95. Levron, *Pierre Mauclerc*, p. 177. Haut-Jussé, *Les papes et les ducs de Bretagne*, I, 112, note 3.

[2] "Cartulaire de Rays," *Archives historiques du Poitou*, XXVIII (1898), cxxx-cxxxiii.

[3] Morice, *Preuves*, I, 797.

[4] In 1225, some four years before Hugh's death, he and Margaret stated clearly that they had no children. *Cartulaires du Bas-Poitou*, p. 192.

none of her inheritance to her son. While the uncertainty surrounding the exact nature of Margaret's right to the baronies of La Garnache and Montaigu prevents this proof from being absolutely conclusive, in combination with the other evidence it seems sufficient to establish the fact that Oliver was not the son of Margaret and Peter.

Thus there is no sound reason for not accepting the epitaph quoted by Blanchard and making Oliver the son of Dame Nicole. This conclusion immediately brings forward the question of his legitimacy. M. Piet believed that he was a bastard, but Blanchard with true chivalry points out that there is no evidence strong enough to justify aspersions on Nicole's virtue. While it is indeed impertinent for a historian to probe the chastity of a fair lady of the past, I cannot but believe that M. Blanchard's chivalry is misplaced and that Nicole yielded to Peter without the formalities of a wedding. One must, of course, lay aside the consideration that there is no evidence whatever that Peter had a third wife. An argument from silence must not be used to question a lady's virtue. But it is extremely difficult to find a time when Peter could have married Nicole. It is true that he was a widower from the death of Alix in 1221 to his marriage to Margaret in 1230, but in 1226 he planned to wed Jeanne of Flanders and in 1229 Alix of Cyprus. Although it is not impossible that Peter might have fitted a short period of wedded life into those nine years, his general conduct was that of a heart-free bachelor. There is, however, a still better reason for doubting Oliver's legitimacy—he inherited none of his father's lands except the barony of Machecoul to which Peter had no real claim. Peter's sister Isabel gave Oliver part of the revenues which had been settled on her by her husband Count John of Roucy.[5] For the rest he was obliged to live on what he could retain from his father's usurpation of Machecoul. Now it is, of course, clear that even if he were legitimate Oliver would have had no claim to any part of Brittany, but it is inconceivable that Peter would not have given him some share in his other fiefs.

[5] Duchesne, *Maison de Dreux*, p. 330.

In summary one can only say that our knowledge of Oliver's origin is most unsatisfactory. He was certainly not the son of Margaret, and there seems little doubt that his mother's name was Nicole. He may have been Peter's legitimate son and Nicole the duke's chaste wife, but the available evidence tends to support the contrary view.

M. Levron has written a very pleasant passage based on the belief that Peter wrote the chanson " Nouviaument m'est pris envie de bien amer par amors " for Margaret of Montaigu.[6] When one considers that Margaret was certainly thirty-nine and probably somewhat older when Peter married her, this seems most improbable. If one chooses not to accept the apparently overwhelming evidence presented by M. Bédier to prove that John of Brittany rather than Peter wrote the chansons ascribed to *Li quens de Bretaigne,* it would seem that Dame Nicole might well be credited with inspiring this poem.[7]

---

[6] Levron, *Pierre Mauclerc,* pp. 174-177.

[7] Joseph Bédier, " Les chansons du comte de Bretagne," *Mélanges de linguistique et de littérature offerts à Alfred Jeanroy* (Paris, 1928), pp. 477-481.

APPENDIX IV

CREDITOR OR DEBTOR?

While it is impossible to establish a balance sheet for Peter's contest with the French crown and so prove or disprove M. Levron's assertion that the duke exhausted the resources of Brittany in the futile struggle, one can easily show that the calculations on which that scholar based his opinion were completely erroneous. M. Levron believed that the large sums of money which Henry III gave to Peter were in repayment of loans which the duke had made to the king.[1] There is no basis whatever for this view. The English chancery was extremely precise in its phraseology, and it had developed set formulas for referring to loans. Peter did make several small loans to Henry, and the documents which mention them leave no doubt as to the nature of these transactions.[2] But the letters patent of October 8, 1230, which Levron accepted as a promise by Henry to repay a loan of 6,000 marks contain none of the phrases which the chancery used in speaking of loans.[3] In fact when the agreement of September 23 by which Henry undertook to pay a body of troops in Peter's service is considered, it becomes clear that the 6,000 marks must have been intended as a first installment on their wages.[4] This is confirmed by a note in the liberate rolls regarding the financial convention made between Henry and Peter in April 1233—"Memorandum, that the king made fine with the count of Brittany for 10,000 marks for all debts and arrears that the king owed to him of the agreement made between them concerning a number of knights...to be found by the count in times of peace and of war."[5] In short

[1] Catalogue, pp. 190-191; Pierre Mauclerc, pp. 117, 188.
[2] c marcas et L libras quas P. comes Britannie regi accomodavit. Close rolls, 1227-1231, p. 517. L libras sterlingorum quas mutuo recepimus de denariis ipsius ducis. Patent rolls, 1225-1232, p. 408.
[3] Sciatis quod de VI milibus marcarum quas debemus dilecto et fideli nostro P. duci Britannie et comiti Richemundie, tenemur ei reddere.... Ibid., p. 403.
[4] Ibid., p. 399.
[5] Calendar of liberate rolls, 1226-1240, p. 239.

M. Levron's calculations were in error by at least 15,000 marks or £10,000 sterling—a sum equal to about £30,000 of Paris and exceeding by £3,000 of Paris the net annual revenue of the county of Champagne. This magnificent mistake would alone make his opinion of Peter's financial status at the end of the war absolutely worthless. It is, however, impossible to resist the temptation to give one more example of M. Levron's technique in dealing with financial matters. In discussing Henry III's sojourn in Nantes in the summer of 1230 he states " Le 7 juin, il [Henry] demanda au duc de lui faire expédier vingt mille des carreaux (monnaie de compte) déposés au château de Rennes. Somme considérable. Comptait-il, avec cet argent, acheter la fidélité des seigneurs Poitevins? " [6] This statement is clearly based on letters close of June 7, 1230, which read as follows—*Mandatum est comiti Britannie quod mitti faciat ad dominum regem usque Nonetas XX milia quarellorum de quarellis domini regis qui sunt in castro suo apud Resnes.*[7] Obviously the *XX milia quarellorum* are 20,000 cross-bow bolts or quarrels. This incredible error on M. Levron's part can be explained in only one way. In M. Berger's *Blanche de Castille* there appear two illuminating sentences. " Le 7 juin, il [Henry III] demande à Pierre Mauclerc vingt mille carreaux qu'il a déposés dans le château de Rennes. En mai, en juillet, en août, en septembre, il se fait envoyer de l'argent." [8] Berger was, of course, fully aware that a carreau was not a money of account, but one can easily see how M. Levron became confused.[9] These samples of M. Levron's accuracy in research seem to me sufficient not only to discredit his account of the financial relations between Peter and Henry III but also to justify my course in completely ignoring his *Pierre Mauclerc*. They are, however, merely two tidbits chosen from a large supply of similar delicious morsels.

[6] *Pierre Mauclerc*, p. 113.
[7] *Close rolls, 1227-1231*, p. 414.
[8] *Blanche de Castille*, pp. 170-171.
[9] On a later page M. Berger makes clear his conception of the meaning of carreaux. " Le maire et la commune de Bordeaux furent avertis...d'envoyer à leur prince, pour les arbalétriers, trente-mille de ses carreaux." *Ibid.*, p. 180. In this case also the Latin form was *quarellorum*. *Close rolls, 1227-1231*, p. 422.

INDEX

147

GENEALOGICAL CHART I

House of Dreux

Robert I, (a) count of Dreux, d. 1188.
m. (2) Hawise of Evreux, widow of Rotrou I, count of Perche.
    (3) Agnes of Baudemont, widow of Milo II, count of Bar-sur-Seine.(b)

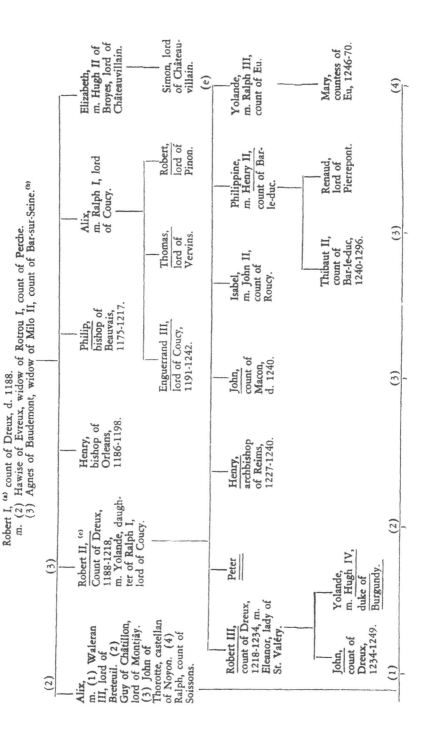

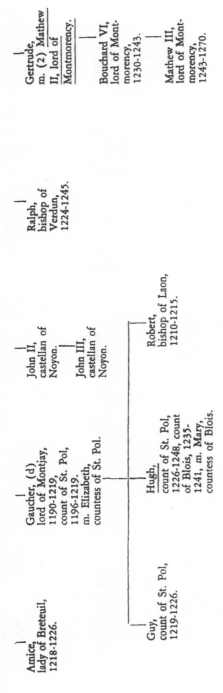

(a) This chart is based on Mas Latrie, *Trésor de chronologie d'histoire et de géographie* (Paris, 1889).

(b) Agnes brought the county of Braine to the house of Dreux.

(c) The names underscored indicate men who are of particular importance to Peter's biography.

(d) It is not certain that Gaucher was Alix's son. See A. de Dion, "Les seigneurs de Breteuil en Beauvaisis," *Mémoires de la société de l'histoire de Paris et de l'Ile-de-France*, X (1883), 214. If M. de Dion is correct in his quotation of an unpublished charter, Gaucher was the son of Guy of Châtillon by his first wife.

(e) Here, as in other parts of this chart, a number of children have been omitted. Sons who never attained important feudal positions and daughters who did not marry men of political importance have been excluded.

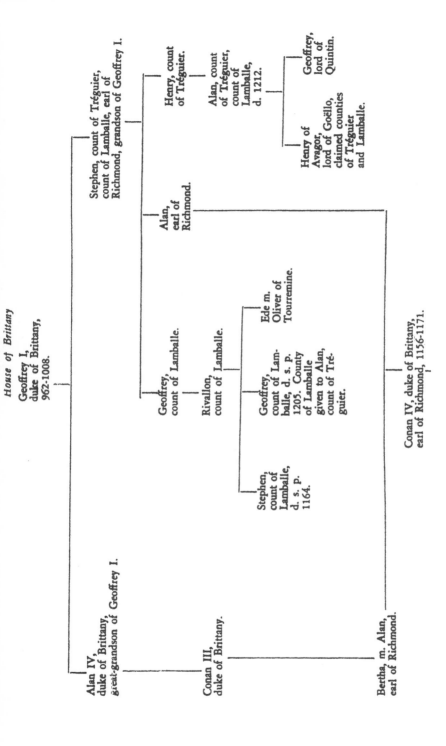

House of Brittany

Geoffrey I,
duke of Brittany,
962-1008.

Alan IV,
duke of Brittany,
great-grandson of Geoffrey I.

Stephen, count of Tréguier,
count of Lamballe, earl of
Richmond, grandson of Geoffrey I.

Henry, count
of Tréguier.

Alan, count
of Tréguier,
count of
Lamballe,
d. 1212.

Geoffrey,
lord of
Quintin.

Henry of
Avagor,
lord of Goëllo,
claimed counties
of Tréguier
and Lamballe.

Alan,
earl of
Richmond.

Geoffrey,
count of Lamballe.

Rivallon,
count of Lamballe.

Ede m.
Oliver of
Tourremine.

Geoffrey,
count of Lam-
balle, d. s. p.
1205. County
of Lamballe
given to Alan,
count of Tré-
guier.

Conan IV, duke of Brittany,
earl of Richmond, 1156-1171.

Conan III,
duke of Brittany.

Stephen,
count of
Lamballe,
d. s. p.
1164.

Bertha, m. Alan,
earl of Richmond.

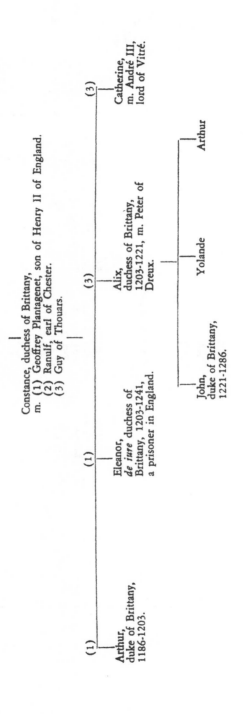

Constance, duchess of Brittany,
m. (1) Geoffrey Plantagenet, son of Henry II of England.
   (2) Ranulf, earl of Chester.
   (3) Guy of Thouars.

(1)
Arthur,
duke of Brittany,
1186-1203.

(1)
Eleanor,
de iure duchess of
Brittany, 1203-1241,
a prisoner in England.

(3)
Alix,
duchess of Brittany,
1203-1221, m. Peter of
Dreux.

John,
duke of Brittany,
1221-1286.

Yolande

Arthur

(3)
Catherine,
m. André III,
lord of Vitré.

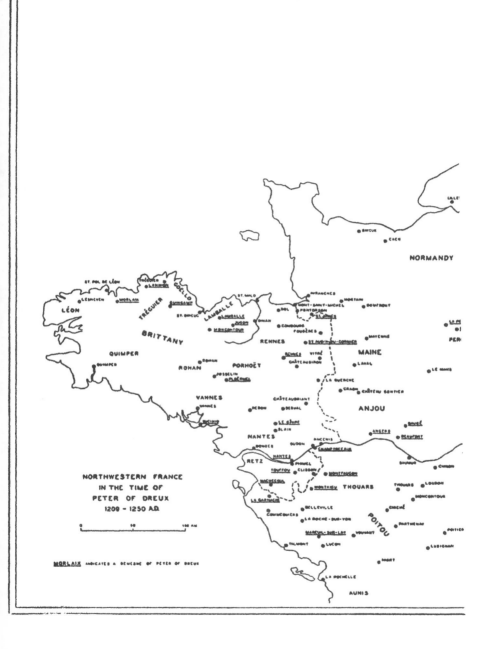

NORTHWESTERN FRANCE
IN THE TIME OF
PETER OF DREUX
1208 – 1250 A.D.

0   50   100 KM

MORLAIX INDICATES A DEMESNE OF PETER OF DREUX

NORMANDY

LÉON

ST. POL DE LÉON

LESNEVEN   MORLAIX

TRÉGUIER   GOËLLO

TRÉGUIER   SUNISAMP

ST. BRIEUC   LAMBALLE

LAMBALLE

DINAN

ST. MALO

QUIMPER   ROHAN   PORHOËT

ROHAN

VANNES

JOSSELIN
PLOËRMEL

VANNES

REDON   DERVAL

LE GÂVRE
BLAIN

NANTES

RETZ

NANTES   PONREL

TOUFFOU   CLISSON

MACHECOUL

LA GARNACHE

COMMEQUIERS   BELLEVILLE

LA ROCHE-SUR-YON

MAREUIL-SUR-LAY   VOUVANT

TALMONT   LUÇON

LA ROCHELLE

AUNIS

BRITTANY

RENNES

COMBOURG   DOL

FOUGÈRES

RENNES   VITRÉ

CHÂTEAUBIRON

CHÂTEAUBRIANT

OUDON   ANCENIS
CHAMPTOCEAUX

MONTAIGU   THOUARS

AVRANCHES   MORTAIN
MONT-SAINT-MICHEL   DOL-FRONT
PONTORSON
ST. JAMES

ST. AUBIN-DU-CORMIER

MAINE

LAVAL

LA GUERCHE

CRAON   CHÂTEAU GONTIER

ANJOU

ANGERS   BAUGÉ

BEAUFORT

SAUMUR   CHINON

THOUARS   LOUDON

MONCONTOUR

CHICHÉ

PARTHENAY   POITIERS

LUSIGNAN

NIORT

BAYEUX   CAEN

MAYENNE

LE MANS

POITOU

MONTAIGU

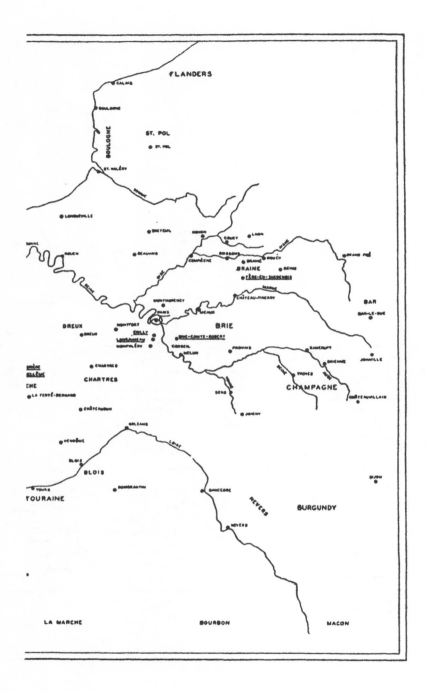

Lightning Source UK Ltd.
Milton Keynes UK
UKHW041527040320
359755UK00001B/29